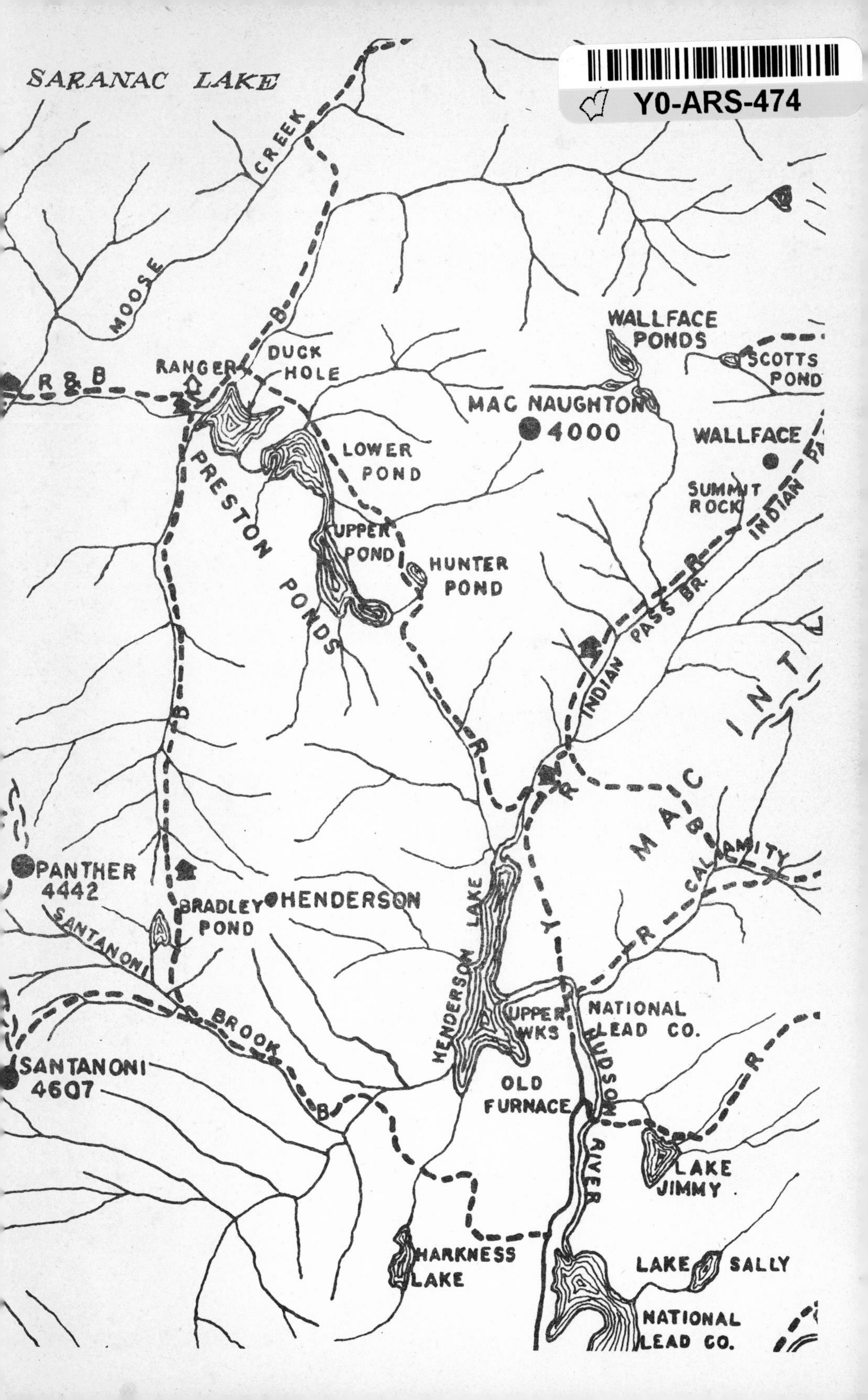
SARANAC LAKE
MOOSE CREEK
R & B
RANGER
DUCK HOLE
PRESTON PONDS
LOWER POND
UPPER POND
HUNTER POND
MAC NAUGHTON
4000
WALLFACE PONDS
SCOTTS POND
WALLFACE
SUMMIT ROCK
INDIAN PASS BR.
CALAMITY
PANTHER
4442
HENDERSON
BRADLEY POND
SANTANONI BROOK
SANTANONI
4607
HENDERSON LAKE
UPPER WKS
NATIONAL LEAD CO.
HUDSON RIVER
OLD FURNACE
LAKE JIMMY
HARKNESS LAKE
LAKE SALLY
NATIONAL LEAD CO.

NOAH JOHN RONDEAU
Adirondack Hermit

Very best wishes –
Maitland C. DeSormo

To: Clifford Smith
From
Mom.

NOAH JOHN RONDEAU

ADIRONDACK HERMIT

MAITLAND C. DE SORMO

NORTH COUNTRY BOOKS
Box 463 — Saranac Lake, N. Y. 12983

First Printing — October, 1969
Second Printing — January, 1970

PRINTED IN THE UNITED STATES OF AMERICA
BY THE WILLARD PRESS, BOONVILLE, N. Y.

To Sue — With sincere
appreciation for countless
hours of digital labor
on this script.

TABLE OF CONTENTS

LIST OF ILLUSTRATIONS

Preface

Just about every person who tries to write for publication frequently finds himself faced with the problem of locating sufficient information to make the compositional agony worthwhile. Seldom is the author fortunate enough to be able to feel that he has access to an abundance of material which lacks little in either quantity or quality. Yet that was exactly what happened in this particular literary effort.

The first break came early last September, when Linda Champagne Hart told me that she had interviewed Noah John in the Lake Placid Hospital during what turned out to be his terminal illness. While talking with him she had seen several of his journals and had been permitted to glance at them.

Since over a year had already elapsed from the time of the interview, she wondered what had happened to the diaries and suggested that I try to find out. Shortly afterward I learned that Chester Rondeau, Noey's nephew and executor, had taken the material to his home in Black Brook.

By contacting him there and with the active assistance of Bill Petty, long-time friend of Noey; Chester and his mother, Mrs. William Rondeau, generously allowed me—acting in behalf of the Lake Placid-North Elba Historical Society—to take the material and do what I could to write a book about the Hermit.

Then, when I had looked over the cartons, I found that Noey's literary legacy contained not only his combination journal-scrapbooks, his poems and some correspondence but also a handwritten 121 page gem which he had entitled "Recollections of 60 years." Right at that point I felt that I had already been given a providentially fine head start.

I have left this lead-off section practically untouched—in order to retain the full flavor of Noah's thought processes and his remarkable way with words.

I also realize full well that there are many loose ends and unexplained phases relating especially to his early boyhood and intra-family relationships. Regrettably, in spite of persistent efforts to resolve some of the anticipated reader questions, I have been unable to satisfy my own curiosity about these admittedly pertinent details. Just one such question would be: "Isn't it strange that the Corrow and Rondeau families did not attend Maggie's wedding? Since Noah does not provide the answer and since all the principals are long since dead, we will never know the reason—unless, plausibly, Maggie's mother felt that cooking the wedding supper was more important than the wedding service itself.

This is just one of many hazy areas. Another is the mother-son relationship. Alice Corrow Rondeau, who died in January 1901, only three years after Noah ran away from home, was apparently never close to her oldest son, who years afterward told one of his closest friends that he always considered his Aunt Maggie to have been more of a mother to him than his real mother. Noah's attitude toward and opinion of his father is made unmistakably obvious. And these are only two of several such unsolved areas that would indicate at least some brotherly concern.

One of the many legends about N. J. R. concerns the time his sister, Maggie Rondeau Wilcox, was seriously shot. The Forest Rangers insist on the accuracy of the story of how a friend hiked 22 miles to inform Noah of her accident. It was dusk when he arrived. "Where'd they take her?" asked Noah. "Hospital in Lake Placid" was the friend's answer. Noah picked up the lantern, told his visitor to make himself to home—and was off on the 50-mile trek to the hospital. On arrival he found she had died.

Knowing that Noah had for many years been an

honorary member of both the Adirondack Mountain Club and the 46ers, I knew that source material collecting would be primarily a matter of contacting those who had frequently visited the Hermit at his bailiwick overlooking the lovely Cold River Valley—friends of his who considered him to be a rather special sort of person. Later on I received ample evidence that many other people also shared that same high opinion of him.

The response was almost immediate and most encouraging: Dr. Adolph Dittmar of Morrisonville, N.Y.; Grace Hudowalski of Albany and Schroon Lake (Adirondack, N.Y.); Dorothy and Nell Plum of Keene; the Drs. C. V. Latimer and his son of Deposit and Hudson Falls respectively; Barney Fowler of the Albany *Times Union* and Harold Brown, editor of the Malone *Evening Telegram*. To these I am very grateful for information.

Of equal help were Noah's long-time friends: Frank Blanchard of Otisville; Ross Freeman of Corey's; Oscar Burguiere of Las Vegas, Nevada; Alphonse Beaudette of Tupper Lake; Madeline Dodge of Wilmington and Dick Smith of Lake Placid, owner of Singing Pines at Wilmington, where Noah spent the last three years of his life.

I am also indebted to Marjorie Porter of Keeseville, Peggy Byrne of Plattsburgh, and Mrs. Muriel Whittum of Corey's.

Mrs. Edward Harmes, Sr. of Binghamton and Walton Huestis and Cleon Bump of Chestertown each made available photos which helped enhance the book.

I acknowledge my special appreciation to Albert Bromley, Director of Division of Conservation Education of the New York State Conservation Department, who gave me permission to use Clayt Seagears' fine article and two of his Cold River photos.

All of us have derived a great deal of pleasure and satisfaction from our participation in this team effort to perpetuate the memory of a truly memorable man—Noah

John Rondeau, the Hermit—Mayor of Cold River City, Population 1. (Town of Newcomb).

Introduction

Since the following clever article served as the spotlight which first focused nation-wide attention on the hermit of Cold River, it provides a most appropriate introduction for this opus.

THE HERMIT OF COLD RIVER

by CLAYT SEAGEARS

Reprinted from October-November 1946 New York State *Conservationist.*

There isn't a more bonafide hermit in the whole United States—including Sharktooth Shoal—than Noah John Rondeau, who has occupied a hole in a woodpile way the hell and gone back in the Adirondack wilderness for 33 years.

Noah John is not only the real McCoy in the hermit department; he looks like hermits are supposed to look. He lives the same way.

He has himself a Sunday suit fabricated out of a couple of deer hides and assembled with bear-tooth toggles. He hunts. He fishes. He uses the longbow. He keeps a diary in secret code and sets his calendar by the stars. He owns less household equipment than a Tenderfoot Scout would take on an overnight hike, and how he gets through a long, zero Adirondack winter in that layout of his is strictly a lesson in hibernation which any woodchuck would do well to look into.

Noah John is, in truth, spang out of this universe.

Perhaps we shouldn't wait to give out with a rich moral. We have a State with darned near 14 million people in it, the teemingest population in the nation. Yet here's a guy wanting to be a hermit who was able to be one with a minimum of outside interference, and in a peak-studded wilderness six hours by forest foot-trail from the nearest hamlet. The moral thus seems to be that (1) Noah John is one in 14 million and (2) that despite a population density of 250 folks per square mile we still have large quantities of country for people to lose themselves in when pressed (for various reasons) for a walk in spaces very wide and very wild.

Leave us draw up a hunk of balsam stump while Noah John cooks what very well may turn out to be his whole day's "vittles"—a few flapjacks bogged down with his own brand of syrup.

This cooking function is performed (in summer) over a more or less perpetual open fire. He flaps the jacks in bear grease, rolls them up like a cigar, bites off about up to the band and then takes a healthy swig of syrup out of a bottle still ketchupy around the seams. Nuts, says Noah, to the napkin trade.

And let us gaze (withal, with awe) upon the unique living quarters of Noah John. What appear to be wooden tepees in the photo on the next page are indeed wooden tepees—but of a variety more practical than anything ever described in the Manual of Carpentry and Tinkers for Growing Boys. Noah John lives in his own woodpile. Come Spring, he has burned his kitchenette, his storage vault, his front parlor and his powder room behind him. Furthermore, he has made it easy to do.

The system is this: When Winter has run itself out down the mountain rivers, Noah John starts building up his tepee village. He cuts long poles of efficient burning diameter. Every three feet he notches them nearly through. Then he stacks 'em up like a wigwam, leaving an interior recess large enough to stretch out in. Thus, when winter has piled the drifts high and our hermit's activity has been reduced to a minimum, the chore of keeping a fire is a cinch. Noah John merely reaches out the door, removes a pole, gives it a belt with the axe head, and the notched pieces fall apart. He admits it took him a few years to figure out the proper deal for this easy-living angle; but what do a few years amount to in a pattern of life such as his?

Noah John is 63 years old. He now finds it bad news to do his main sleeping under a drafty canopy of slanted poles. So he had a hovel made from a few boards off a long defunct lumber camp. Over the so-called door to this realm of retirement the old boy has nailed up a sign "TOWN HALL." Inside there's just room enough for a sort of bed and a crude stove. Every year the place gets smaller, due to encroachment of soot layers from the walls. On the bed is just what you'd expect to find on the bed of a better class hermit—a bear skin. The interior has touches here and there of gaudy decor—the stalagmite drippings of myriad red, yellow and white candles. There are no windows and none are necessary, because the occupant is, perforce, always close to the door. It's as simple as that.

He has another cubbyhole for the convenience of visiting firemen—the hikers who occasionally call on him. This jointed shelter does have a window, and more extensive decoration—the chalky shoulder blades of a dozen beavers, the antlers of bygone bucks and the skulls of two degreased bears. These rattle nicely in the breeze and add to the general cheer.

Noah John, despite his 33 long years of complete isolation, and despite the primitive aspects of his existence, is by no means uncouth or illiterate. By any yardstick of human behavior he is a distinctly bright gent. It would be difficult, in fact, to find a single button missing, except on his pants. He loves to talk—picturesque hermit talk if he thinks his hiker-visitor would be made any happier by it. He reads anything he can lay hands on, but leans to books on astronomy, philosophy and kindred subjects of the solitudes. This is quite understandable.

He likes people, (if they don't crowd him), but it is suspected that he views them with some suspicion. Inherently honest himself, Noah John hints darkly that it was a sequence of sharp practices by others, when he was the youthful proprietor of a barber chair, which drove him from what he felt was a chiseling world to the honesty of the open spaces.

Noah John's outdoors is built to order for a hermit. His spot is on a bluff high over the end of Cold River Flow, twelve miles as the crow flies south of Lower Saranac Lake, ten miles northeast of Long Lake Village and twenty miles west of Keene Valley. Trails maintained by the Conservation Department lead all the way—about nineteen miles of hiking in any direction, except that eleven miles can be made by canoeing to the north end of Long Lake, thence into the Raquette and then a mile or so up the Cold. Most hikers go in via Long Lake Village and Shattuck Clearing, although some prefer the hoof route via Corey's (just south of Upper Saranac) and Mountain Pond. Four miles to Noah John's east are Preston Ponds, nestling at the end of Indian Pass. He couldn't have picked a more isolated place to live with an Ouija board.

Nor could he have picked a spot of greater beauty. Towering across Noah's valley is Panther Mountain, and Santanoni and Henderson. Behind him rear Seymour, Seward and the Sawtooths. He lives on a strip of lumber company holdings in the middle of a huge chunk of State land comprising about 130 square miles.

It's wild land, a stronghold of marten and fisher. Noah used to run a 40-mile trap line when he was more spry. Now he has all he can do to "come out" once a year for a packbasket of staples. Forest Rangers—like Orville Betters or Wayne Tyler—or deer hunters and hikers bring him his mail now and then, plus small supplies of food. Or Fred McLane, the Conservation Department's head plane pilot, may drop him bread and papers. Maybe the brook trout are biting in Noah John's Lost Pond or in Cold River Flow. Maybe a snowshoe rabbit rams its head against Noah John's sitting log and conks out conveniently in time for a lonely, February meal. Maybe.

The Conservation Department has a great friend in Noah John. Spry or not—if anything went wrong in the woods he'd be out of there on all two cycles to tell the boys about it. He's a great friend of Man in General, too. For he's the magnet which lures many a hiker deep into some of the grandest country in the world, and that kind of stuff is good for what ails you.

Yep, everything considered, there's quite a guy behind all that alfalfa.

RECOLLECTIONS OF SIXTY YEARS

By Noah John Rondeau

A French Wedding in a Log House in 1890

It was New Year's Eve in 1889: I was in the first half of my seventh year and Mother gave me an evening bath and as I remember it the program of oncoming New Year's Day was causing a new atmosphere to prevail in our Kitchen, and that together with Mother's special maneuvers made the bath a semi-special ablution. And after the bath I was tucked into Bed.

It was in the old Dewyer House on Jackson Hill; four miles easterly from the Fork of the Ausable River and among the Sylvan Hills of Clinton County. And I slept through the transitional night that closed the Gay Eighties and launched the New Nineties; little did I guess or dream about what New Year's Day had in store. I was presumely too young to be told or to appreciate and for the most part, even to comprehend the preparations which were being made to celebrate a French Happy New Year Day. Which had all the usual Program plus a very Special Climax to justify the anticipation and fulfillment of a Best Ever New Year Day.

The Special Climax: My Mother's Sister Maggie Corrow, a Beautiful Maiden in her twenty-fourth year, was to celebrate the twenty-fourth January—First of Her Life by becoming the Wife of Henry Miner Jr. of Ausable Forks.

And as I understood in after years, Henry Miner had already made arrangements with Sid Benway, a Fiddler of the time, to come with his Fiddle and Rosin and Bow and render Music during the night, to prompt Quadrille, French Four Jig Dancing.

And in that day Gasoline Stations and Automobiles were as scarce as Teddy Bears and Merry Widow Hats. But there were Livery Stables with Fleet Horses "For Hire." And Henry Miner Jr. and His Dad—Henry Miner Sr., Each had arranged at the Livery for a Prancing Horse, a Winter Cutter, Colorful Robes and Tassels and Jangling Bells, for a four mile drive in the winding valley for the Marriage Ceremony at the Church and back to the Bride's Home for a Merry Joyful Afternoon, a Wedding Supper and All Night Dance.

And in the Bride's Home of Primitive Rustic Log Dwelling, more preparations had been made; the Bride's Wedding Dress, much the work of Her Own Hands, and a Bridal Veil and all that is required to make a Beautiful Finished Trousseau was now complete and waiting.

And My Grand Mother, Marie-Antoinette Corrow, had made the Wedding Cake. And the bottom stratum was bigger than the Apparent Full Moon is to Natural Vision and The Cupola Top was a Cup Cake that constituted The Seventh Story. And the mounting Consentric Wedding Cake was skilfully coated with Confection Frosting in Polly Colors and Inlaid with hundreds of Tiny Candies and further Ornamented with Dandy Roses. And it was a Self-Explanatory and Complimentary Witness to the Cook who made it.

And Modern Steamer Trunks were scarce in Gram's Log House in 1889 and for ever before and after. But there were several Ward Robe Chests that were made of Broad Boards of White Pine and Cedar. The making of some of the Boards in an earlier day was Hand Work with a Broad Axe. And the making of the Chest was invariably the handiwork of illiterate Frenchmen who made their Own Hard Wood Pegs to retap Their Coarse Boots. They also raised and cured Their Own Tobacco; And they Lit Their Loaded Pipes by thrashing a Spark from a piece of Flint, on a piece of Maple Punk and then blowing on the Spark and generating a Little Live Coal with which to light the Calumet for all occasions.

At the time of which I write, Punk and Flint as the Ignition Apparatus of days gone by was in the transition of being, "Put off the Stage" by "Portland and Star Sulphur Matches." But it was still being used.

On that occasion, one of the chests was emptyed of its contents; The Ward Robes, a Powder Horn and a Key Winding Watch were put away elsewhere; and The Wedding Cake was placed in the Chest, and the Chest was set against the Log Wall of The Living Room and Covered with a New Fringed Lap Robe. The reason for putting The Wedding Cake in a Chest was because the Cake was so tall, and so broad at the base that there was not enough horizontal or perpendicular space between any two shelves in Gram's Big Blue Cup Board to accommodate it. And a score of minor preparations were made including the Semi-Annual Application of White Wash on the Old Log Walls.

My Old French Catholic Ancestry regarded Christmas about as They did Sunday; but there were no Special Celebrations and They seem to never have made an acquaintance with Mr. Claus or Sanctimonious Nick. At times They went to Church and once in a few Moons, the subject came up in Their Conversation, that—"The Son of God was born on The First Christmas Day." But they only seemed to know two or three things for certain about that occasion. And when the subject came up on Christmas Day,—especially after They had been to Church, so that They had Their Fine Boots on, They spoke with such confidence, Historically, that a listener was sure to discern and detect, They were the "Wise men" who took "Gifts and Compliments" to The Stable at Bethlehem and made Prophecies on the First Christmas Morning. The Outstanding Day for French Celebrating was New Year's Day; And it was "The Little God" who brought Good Things through The Stove Pipe—and filled Little French Red Stockings that hung on Square Nails and Wooden Pegs.

But in 1890, even The Little God was very Poor among Miners of Raw Iron and Producers of Char Coal, about Jackson Hill and Palmer Hill. At that time, I never knew Him to bring An Aluminum Kettle, a Toy Air Plane or even a Little Ten Cent Automobile. He had Iron Caldrons, Brass Candle Molds and Plain Heavy Earthen Dishes; And He still had in Stock, a very few Large Spinning Wheels to convert Fleecy Wool into Yarn; And He had Smaller Spinning Wheels to Spin Linen Thread from Flax. And for Little Boys and Little Girls who were especially Good, He had Big Sticks of White Candy with Red Stripes and Peanuts that He had been too lazy even to Shuck.

I am not even certain that He came through The Stove Pipe; It was enough to know that He came, as The Peanuts bear evidence. And even in 1890, He was old enough to know enough to go into a House and go out again without waking up People for a few Peanuts in the Shucks.

And without Marble or Mahogany was The Old Dewyer House on Jackson Hill where I was born in 1883 and lived for the first fifteen years of my life; It was built many years before The Eighties and according to The Plan of Long ago. The Frame was of Big Square Timbers that were fitted together with Mortises and Tenons, and held fast and secure with Wooden Pins. The long Dimension of the House was set East and West, and each Gable had a Window; And in the center of The Chamber there was a Square Timber Frame that held up a Short

Chimney of Common Reddish Bricks. The Ceiling in part was The Pole Rafters; and The Elegant Slanting Panel between the Rafters were the Rough Boards of the Roof. And the Apex of the Two Sided Ceiling remained so and slowly put on Deeper Brown according to the years.

And at times, Spiders Ornamented the Corners with their Trap Nets, from which they had their Silken Thread to descend and ascend—Perhaps to drive flies and then go up and tend to the Trap. The Lower part of the ceiling from the Plate up as high as could be reached from a Chair, was papered with newspapers and remnants of Wall Paper in variety. And the side wall finish was the inside surface of the Square Timbers and the Points of the Wooden Pins.

And in the Northwest Corner of my first Home there was the most wonderful set of Stairs that I ever saw until after the Gay Eighties of the nineteenth Century; They went both ways,—up and down. When I was upstairs, they went down; And when I went down they went back up again, and when I went upstairs, I could not go up again until I went down once. The Stairs were too narrow for two-way traffic, so I never went up or down at the same time. But by using good judgement, alternatively, I went up and down many, many times.

And those Stairs possessed another architectural wonder. They were not an Atom too short or too long; according to their slant, they reached exactly from the top of the Kitchen Floor to the Chamber. And even before the end of the nineties I had a surmise: that perhaps the designer of the Stairs might be one of my Ancestors, who presumely had been Self Delighted to go among the Hebrews in the possession of Judah for the first Christmas Occasion. There he finally matured the plan for the Stairs, from an insinuation He imbibed from the architecture of the Historical Stable of Bethlehem.

This, I never varified for certain, But even if that's exactly what happened, He was not so generous with the width of Stairs as He was about some things. The Hands of His Mittens were always three inches too long; And the Seat of His Home Made Pants, even after He installed Himself with the What-Not—had enough spare room for a Morter Hod and a Bee Hive.

For the old Dewyer House, the space down stairs was divided into three rooms: the West half was a Kitchen and the East half was divided to make two equal Bed Rooms. And under the "Two Way Stairs" encased in the Kitchen Corner, there were Stairs that went down into a small cellar that had natural ground for a Floor. And in the northeast Corner there was a splendid Spring of Clear Cold Water.

And out-of-doors was more spacious and there I had many a First. There were several acres of Clearing and beyond were the Woods and Varied Kaleidoscopic Scenes. The Clearing had rough Meadow Land that produced Hay for a Cow and a few Sheep. And there was a generous Garden of Vegetables and field of Corn and potatoes; And a dozen varieties of Garden Flowers. And also a score of Apple Trees that bear a variety of common apples. Choke Cherries, Black Cherries and a variety of Acorns and Berries grew abundantly.

There I had my own first Garden that was not over six feet square. There, experience and observation taught that Potatoes planted in the Ground for a season, multiplied. And an Egg, set under a Hen for three weeks, was a Downy Chicken and two semi Egg Shells. My little Bossy Calf in two or three years was a Mother Cow.

There I heard my first Bird-Song, found my first Bird's Nest and chased my first Chipmunk; Saw my first Woodchuck on the Wall. And planted my first Lilac Bush and Sweet-Flag Roots. There I found my first Trailing Arbutus the day I found my first Snail Shell. There I caught my first Red Squirrel and White Weasel in a Steel Trap, and my first Snow-Shoe Rabbit in a Snare, made of Copper Wire.

I had all, and more, than Whittier's "Bare Foot Boy:"—comparatively—all that was lacking was "The Sand Rimmed Pickerel Pond." And in the middle of the nineties I found it, four miles away—At that time "Slush Pond," now "Fern Lake."

The Road on Jackson Hill had been laid out East and West and passed within a hundred feet on the north side of the House. And each way from Home lived my nearest neighbor within a mile: To the East,—John Breen and to the West—Billy Peckham. And both were very old Men when I was a little Boy; And both lived in very old Log Houses; and both were Old Settlers who had come from The Green Fields of Ireland many years before I was born.

And to the north elevated Dewyer Hill, a small Mountain with Summit within a mile of my six foot Garden; but at that time it was far beyond the radius of my explorations: nevertheless. north was positively up hill. And to the South, continued, topographically with moderation.

The Road was old for years, and primitive in style: In the middle of the Road Stones projected to twenty inches above the surface of the Ground. And Lumber Wagons had Narrow Tires, because Broad Tires were not born until advancing in the Nineties. And most of the Wagons were drawn by Horses, but some were still being hauled by a Yoke of Oxen.

My radius of exploration was a twenty five acre Clearing and about a hundred feet in the Bordering Woods. But never out of sight of The Old Dewyer House. I had seen one House and no more; There were other Houses, but presumely, they were all alike. So much so that if I ever went into another Kitchen, I would need no further Architectural Introduction in order to find the other Compartments—and According to The Unique Homogeneous House Plan, as materialized in the old Dewyer House on Jackson Hill.

If I had ever heard the words "North" or "Cardinal Point" it meant nothing to me. All I had seen of the World slanted one way; And up hill was up hill in that direction as far as I could ever go or imagine. And down hill was the reverse and that too was eternal. And the Central Point between the two eternities—up hill and down hill—was The Old Dewyer House on Jackson Hill.

My Stock in Store did not afford all varieties for debate and comparison. And I had not thought to change the world—not even the slant. So I left it just as it was. And my first four Cardinal Points were "Up Hill, Down Hill, Toward John Breen and Toward Billy Peckham."

There was not much Traffic Trouble on the Road through the Clearing on Jackson Hill, and at times it took a week to bring along a Team of Horses or Yoke of Oxen. And in mild weather when I played out of Doors, when a Yoke of Oxen came along, I stood and gazed until they went out of sight. But in winter, when Snow and cold kept me in the House, I lost some Traffic. There were no windows in the ends of the House except in the Gables; So when I had a warning that "traffic was on" I hurried upstairs to the Window toward Billy Peckham, and watched until the traffic disappeared going by the side of the house that was up hill. And while my Circus was going by the House I ran to the other end of the Chamber, to the Window toward John Breen, and I watched what ever was going until it disappeared, wending its way on the Crooked Road among the Trees.

And while upstairs, I might play an Overture; My first Musical Instrument was there. It was an old fashion, long, rusty Cross Cut Saw, with large triangular Teeth, and it hung on a square spike near the window toward John Breen. Round nails and Spikes were not made yet, so I would take a square Spike and hit the Saw

Blade which rang out Steel Music that vibrated for several seconds after I struck the note.

And my first Home Pets were: An old Black Cat and Mage, a big, strong, brown mongrel Dog, but he use to frighten me with his roaring fights with Billy Peckham's Old Shep.

The Dog Fight

One day, in the last of the Eighties, I was playing on the steps, just out of doors toward Billy Peckham. And Mage set up in the Yard a dozen feet away; And he was gazing down hill in attitude of semi-dormant dream. And I looked up and Billy Peckham was coming with His Cane and Old Shep was trotting along.

Mage was getting along in years and slightly deft; and it seems that on that occasion Billy Peckham might get by unnoticed if it had not been but for Old Shep. But when Billy and Shep got opposite of Mage, Shep made a sprinting race and jumped on Mage before Mage knew anything about it. To say the least, that was an insult, right in Mage's Home Yard, and so the Roaring Fight was on.

Billy Peckham was not very speedy in that day; His Right Knee was stiff and when He stepped over a Log He had to swing His Leg horizontally to put His Foot over the Log. There was no bending of the Knee. And besides, He was in His Eighties. According, He made a Noble Dash toward the Dog Fight. But He was also coming toward me and He had His Cane and He looked furious. And my thought of Billy Peckham, at that time, was not to invite Him to come Head On with a cane.

I had often been told that, "If you go out of your Clearing, Billy Peckham will catch you and eat you up." And "Billy Peckham eats Little Boys—He was driven out of Ireland for eating a dozen of Them."

The Dog Fight was on and Billy Peckham was coming, so I went in the House; And as I went in I met Mother coming out with a Pail of Water to throw on the Dogs. This She accomplished, and at the same time, Billy Peckham arrived and struck Shep a half dozen times with His Cane. And between hits he screamed out some words with Irish Brogue.

My English at that time was all in French; So I won't tell what Billy Peckham said, but I knew from His manipulation of the Cane and the volume and pitch of His vocal expressions that it was very serious for Old Shep. The Pail of Water and the Cane parted the Fighting Dogs. Billy made another lunge at Shep and struck again with the Cane, but that time Shep excaped the Cane and he went back to the Road. Mother stamped Her Foot on the Ground, raised the Empty Water Pail and screamed a positive command to Mage and he went in the House.

I was watching through the Door Way toward Billy Peckham. Mother had a rather limited vocabulary of English with French Accent in every line. Billy Peckham has an equivalent for vocal scope and the best Irish Brogue that ever came from Ireland. Mother and Billy Peckham talked for two minutes after the fight; Then Billy and Shep went on their way toward John Breen.

To me, a Dog fight was a frightful thing: To Mother and Billy Peckham, it was just a little bout between two Old Dogs, whose years had truncated their canines so they could do no damage anyway. And such a bout could happen and did happen in the best neighborhood in all the World.

No doubt Old Shep had some justification when he jumped on Mage; Even when Mage was at home minding his own business and concentrating on a day dream. And Mage certainly had reasons for unpleasant remembrances of Billy Peckham. And accordingly he may have felt under no obligation to keep on Loving Neighborly Terms with Old Shep. Often Mage would go for A Random Scoot in the Woods; Perhaps much like a boy, to see Squirrels and Rabbits. And at times he got as far as Billy Peckham's. Maybe Mage's Pride would not allow him to stay at home all the time and let Shep presume and justify an idea, that "Mage was even afraid to pass by on the Stony Public Road."

And it's not completely without likelihood, or unreasonable, to presume that there may have been a day, when there was a Dog Fight in Billy Peckham's Door Yard as well as at the Old Dewyer House.

And from Billy Peckham's Point of View, Mage may have proven himself a nuisance at times. And Shep may have given his Master no plaudit complimentary recommendation of Mage.

At least, on one occasion, Billy Peckham took His Double Barrel Muzzle Loading Shot Gun; And as Mage headed toward John Breen, Billy Peckham shot and hit Mage in the end toward Billy Peckham. It did not put his Eyes out, but it accelerated his speed. And that day, Mage went home, making A New Time Record; And not unmindful about his End toward Billy Peckham. The sting of the Lead Shots and the audible report of the Gun overtook Mage at the same time and impressed him that the two were associated and he never forgot it.

Mage was forever after afraid of explosive sounds. And when a Thunder Storm came up, which was generally from toward Billy Peckham, at the first sharp crash of Thunder, Old Mage fearfully slunk in the House, and he went in a corner as far as he could get under a Bed. And he stayed there until the Thunder Storm was over. Then he would come out, presumely when his auditories persuaded him that Billy Peckham's wrath and the furiousness of the Shot Gun had abated.

New Year's Day

My first possible recollection of the nineties was an hour before dawn January First, 1890. I was on Mother's Knee in front of the Wood Fire that burned in the Kitchen Stove; And Mother was trying to dress me and wake me up at the same time. She interrogated—"Are you awake?" Perhaps many times before She got an answer; And She may have had an answer before I was conscious of it.

Accordingly, I woke up; But how sleepy I was! I had been taken out of Bed at least two hours before my usual schedule; My Head was heavy and my Neck was limp; I wanted to lay my Head on Mother and sleep! But no, there were other things on the Program, that I knew nothing about. The Little God had brought me a little Black Woolen Cap during the night; And there were strange Garments on Chairs about the Kitchen.

My Dad, Peter Rondeau, occasionally stoked the Stove with Hard Wood chunks. The night was cold, and dark, and about twenty inches of snow covered the Ground. We had a hurried Breakfast of Home Cured Pork, Beans, Bread and Tea. Then there was unusual commotion about the Kitchen for a while. Such as Driving the Cat to the Cellar, and making a Bed in the corner for Mage and pulling down Window Shades.

And for the next change there was noise toward Billy Peckham: Like creaking of Frozen Boards and Sticks; And a squeaking of Heavy Sleighs sliding sidewise in Frosty Snow. And a voice just outside, shouted: "whoa!"

Peter Rondeau opened the Door and screamed out and the strange voice answered just outside. And while the Door was open the Air pressed in and, as it mingled with the Warm Air in the Kitchen, it infused the appearance of Nebulosity; And when it reached me near the Kitchen Stove, it was Winter's Cold Breath.

And in a moment, Grandfather, Charles Corrow, walked in with a Kerosene Lantern in His Hand. There were Hand Shakes and a generous exchange of, "Best Wishes" and "A Happy New Year."

Grandpa Corrow was A Tall Man of sixty-four Happy New Years. He wore A Big Winter Cap and He had Whiskers as big, and as white, as A Winter Snow Shoe Rabbit. And He wore a Big Long Over Coat, Sheepskin Leggins and rather Low Rubbers. And the Little God had brought Him New Leather Mittens with Wooly Fleece Linings.

Grandpa sat near the Stove and there was more commotion in the Kitchen—Donning Winter Caps and Over Coats and tying Sashes and Scarfs.

The next change in the Morning Program: Peter Rondeau took a Pail of Water, and a Dipper and after He had lifted two Griddles off the old Stove, He poured two or three Dippers of Water in the Stove and put out the Fire. Then He took down the Kerosene Lamp and blew out the Light and He set the Lamp back in its bracket on The Wall. And We were left in The Dim Light of Grandpa's Lantern. And immediately we were marching out of The House. Then immediately we stood out of Doors and The Snow squeaked under Our Feet.

Peter Rondeau closed The Door, then he closed a Storm Door on which He put a Pad Lock. And next We were progressively getting into Grandpa Corrow's Sleigh Box: Grandpa had a Good Big Horse and Double Sleighs and a Big Long Box on the Sleighs. And He had Broad Boards, four feet long, to use as Seats across the Box. And in The Box there was a generous spread of Straw and plenty of Blankets.

A Broad Board was set across The Sleigh Box and then a Blanket was spread over The Broad Seat and extended generously forward over the Straw on the Bottom of The Box. Mother sat on the Broad Seat, with a Baby Girl in Her Arms. And five year old Sister and I hugged up on each side of Mother. But it was a cold morning and We were shortly told to "Sit at Mother's Feet on the Blanket on the Straw." Then another Blanket was pulled completely over us and over Mother's Lap. But I wanted to see The Show, and hear the conversation; So I stood up and held my Head over the Blanket.

Dad and Gramp stood in The Front of The Sleigh Box; Dad held the Lantern and Gramp commanded The Big Horses. We made 6 small semi circles about Mage and Shep's Arena, Then We went "Up Hill." The Ground was rough and Stony and there was loud cracking and squeaking of The Frozen Box and Sleigh Beams, as We creaked through The Frosty Snow over The Frozen Ground. And we made a square angle turn and got on the Main Road and so, We were on Our Way toward Billy Peckham.

There was already an insinuation that the first ray of morning light was disspelling the deepest shades of night. And three Adults were earnestly engaged in lively French conversation as morning Dawn was growing.

And with the fast walking Horses in about fifteen minutes, We were going by Billy Peckham. And Among scattered Trees two hundred feet away from the Road,—The Old Log House was perfectly distinguishable in the first on coming dawn of the nineties. And presumptively, Aged Billy Peckham and His Good Faithful Nellie from Ireland and Old Shep were sleeping. And The Old Shot Gun in the corner was as peaceful and silent as the Broom.

And the moment I went by Billy Peckham's I put my distension limit of "West" behind me in the East toward John Breen. And then I was adventuring in the unknown without Cardinal Points—except four—all in the same direction. In fifteen minutes I had traveled completely out of their radius on my first debut away from Home in Prodigality.

We went West, then North, and then East—Altogether about four miles and making three equiangles of a rough square. And the fourth angle to finish the square was a Foot Trail about a mile long, over little Hills, and it reached from Gramp's Log House to My Square Timbers and Wooden Pins.

And as We Traveled over the Snow Road after Day Light had taken possession, Mother saw something, or at least She thought She did; And it went out of sight and They spoke accordingly. So I popped My Head over the Blanket; They were all concentrating their Optic Power in the same direction. So I tuned up: "What is it?" and "I want to see!" and "Where is it? What did you see?"

Mother pointed and said:—"Right there! I don't see it now but it went right back of the Clump of Cats."

I was more anxious: "A Clump of Cats?"

Mother pointed again: "Yes, right there! Can't you see that Clump of Cats?"

I directly applied all my visionary equipment but in vain; the Horse walked out of My Vision's Reach of every Cat. So I started to debate with Mother, but shortly She made me get back under the Blanket; And then I sat on the Straw philosophizing on my disappointment. "A clump of Cats."

Apparently "The Cats" were in plain sight; And three People saw them and I had plenty of time to see them too. And the fact that I did not see them attached a faze of mystery that should be solved. I had left an Old Cat on Jackson Hill; Probably had seen one or two more; But "A Clump?" Never!

It took days to acquire enough philosophy pertaining to cats to bring a Clump of them out of mystery. And it might have taken a few years, if it had not been for my continual returns to Mother with My Interrogative and explanatory debates on the subject of "Cats."

And when "The Clump of Cats" came out of mystery, it was on this wise: I knew one kind of Animal Cats, and That's all the cats there were: And the French term "Chat" (cat) designated many Species, wild and domestic. And "Chat" designated also Willows—especially Pussy Willows. Mother may have caught a glimpse of a Fox, or a similarity, and there is as much likelihood it was something like a bunch of Dry Leaves propelled by the wind over the Snow. Whatever, it disappeared, back of "A Clump of Pussy Willows" and She spoke and pointed accordingly; But the only Cats I knew that morning I could not recognize in a bunch of Whips projecting above the Snow, anymore than in the Snow itself.

During the winter I got a balance on the subject of "Cats," but in doing that—Mentally—I had to evolve a new specie of "Chat" without enlarging my vocal philology. And the following spring I got some Pussy Willow Branches when they were Budded, And I made a very broad examination of the Fuzzy Buds that Mother called "Pete Chat" (Petit Cat or Kitten). I understood but I was still two percent at a loss; And at least one percent in a haze. And that time I had no starting point to make an investigation. It seemed that my dormant characteristics would demand a broader vocal scope for "chat," if "chat" was to be introduced for many species, and two were to have diversity to include Animals and Bushes.

And my bit of haze was felt without words, except "Chat" when I thought of the demarcation between the "chat" that caught MICE and the "chat" that grew Wood Fiber into Whips that congregated into stationary Clumps.

The Scribbler's Hermit Twist may seem laughable and perhaps it is; And of course I was only 6½ years old. But in fifty-four years from that day, I have only changed my mind to confirm: That it would be easier to invent a word once in a while, than to keep discovering New Species and keep designating with an original "Too often applied term." And finally try to explain: For instance —a score of diversities all with the same "Chat."

Nearing Grandpa Corrow's

In due time We reached our destination: We went into a large Clearing and among Pole Fences and through big open Bar Ways. And all the Top Poles of the Fences held up streamlined Bars of Snow ten inches high. And all the Fence Posts according to their size, held up exaggerated Snow Heads that were broader than the Posts. And the Pure White Loaves were so smooth and well finished that they suggested a serenity of fluffy softness and beauty that would make a philosopher wonder in amazement at the Artistic knowledge there must be in Snow Flakes.

On a curve of the Road in the middle of the Clearing we passed among four or five little Log Stables. And in one of the Stables, four Big Cows were eating their morning Hay. They were not to be seen from the Sleigh Box, but each Cow had a big Bell on her neck and each Bell was loud and had a distinct sound from the other Bells. And as we passed close by the Stable the four Cows busy eating breakfast caused the Bells to peal out the most appropriate, casual, timely metallic ringing of New Year Morning Carols that I ever heard.

About a hundred feet beyond the Log Stables we stopped at Grandpa's Door. The Log House was indeed two Log Houses Perhaps built several years apart. They were built end to end and a General Double Sided Roof covered all. And at one end of the Double House, there was an Outside Cellar that was built of Smaller Logs. The House was old and had acquired a Leanto Summer Kitchen and several Nooks and Corners; And the House was lengthy and low and all was decorated with snow, and above the Low Peaked Roof projected a belching Smoking Stove Pipe.

It was indeed a Picturesque Winter Setting. We hurried out of the Sleigh Box. It was a Nice Calm Winter Morning, but just after the Winter Night, the Air was sharp. The Snow was broadly and neatly shoveled out of all Trails about the House, and along a Big pile of Stove Wood. And a Generous Square had been shoveled out just outside the Garden Gate at the corner of the Outside Cellar. The Little Garden Gate of Little Square Pickets and Little Round Peeled Sticks was swung open and well set in the Snow. And the half of the Gate Above the Snow was ornamented with Little Brown Vines, which had entwined Themselves about the Gate as they grew during the previous summer.

Mother picked up two or three Packages She had put in the Sleigh Box on Jackson Hill, and we went through between the Posts of the Ornamented Gate and along a Board Walk that had an inch of Packed Snow on its surface. Again the Snow squeaked under Our Feet as We went along the Outside Cellar and along the Big Logs of the Main House and by a Kitchen Window. And at the End of the Squeaky Walk we went into a Leanto Summer Kitchen, which was a three angle construction of Boards, and with Door, Window and Roof and Floor and well attached to the side of the Log House as a Skillful Articulation.

And as we went into that first Kitchen, Gram, (Marie Antoinette), opened a Low Broad Vermillion Door; And We turned at square angles and went through the Low Broad Door Way through the Big Logs of the House Wall, and Gram closed the Big Vermillion Door against the Cold Atmosphere outside. Then We were by the Warm Fire in Gram's Kitchen in The Old Log House, just before Sun Rise.

An Embarrassing Situation

There was lively conversation. Everyone had Extra Good New Year Wishes, to French Taste, to deliver—in Special Complimentary Manner. And everyone had news and all had Joy and Gladness enough to put Sparks in Their Eyes. And there was much laughter.

And as said of the French and others—"All talked at the same time." But at least it was not just a habit to blab or a mere street gift of gab. Everyone knew what everyone said and everyone answered the right one appropriately at the right time. And not without consideration, to have Their vocal applications complimentary and often accompanied with confirming gesture. And the laughter was not the premeditated rehearsed commercial Radio kind. And besides all that, there were side jobs. We were undoing Toggles and Knots made on Jackson Hill before Day Light, and We were doffing Winter Caps and Over Coats.

It was early and the last Frenchman, Mr. Hubert Geror, was just getting up. And there were chores to finish and Breakfast Dishes and there was great concern. The Big Day had come.

After the first Volley, Gram came to me and She started to make a Love Fuss. She was early in The Sixties, not very tall but rather stout, and She was noticeably blanching and She wore Glasses and for Her years, She was rather Good Looking. She stooped, and looking me in The Eyes, She spoke a few words of Semi-Baby Talk; And when She saw that I was not afraid, She pulled up a Kitchen Chair, and She got me on Her Lap. She hugged me and kissed me and then she began to interrogate:

"Do you Love Gram?"—"Ah—6½? What a Big Man You are!" and "Where did you get your new Cap?"

"The Little God brought it last night," I said.

"Did you see The Little God?"

"No."

"Why didn't You see The Little God?"

"I, I—I was sleeping when He came."

She may have asked a question I knew nothing about; She asked a few more questions and got no answer. So Peter Rondeau brought Himself in, puckering His Eye Brows: "Can't You talk?"

Gram asked another question but I had no answer.

Peter Rondeau tuned His voice low as if entreating as a Tutor discharging a sacred duty: "Can't you answer Gram like a little Man?"

Gram asked another question as if to try the effect of Peter Rondeau's Technique Salve, but the Salve was no good. I was experiencing embarrassment and I tried to get down but Gram held me and She popped another quiz but I was mute. Peter Rondeau suggested to Himself and for the benefit of the Audience: "He's never going to talk anymore."

I got another question and I confirmed Peter Rondeau's prophecy. Gram hugged me and gave me a Love Spank and at the same time she asked two or three questions and She made two or three explanatory clauses, all scrambled together in one semi-quizzical string. And Peter Rondeau suggested to Gram: "The Cats have eaten His tongue." I was near the point of crying, and Dear Gram—She talked as if She had a vocal intake and had lost the Lever to the Shut Off.

Again I tried to get down and that time was successful; so I went from the Kitchen into the Living Room feeling very lackadaisical. I stood alone in the strange Living Room and I was in a Mental Muddle: The strangeness of a multiplicity of material things did not render them without interest.

The Straw Ride over The Snow Road had been perfect—all but "The Clump of Cats"—and that was recorded in my Mental Journal for future reference. The carols by the Bovines were still ringing in my Mental

Auditory and I had a glimpse of the outside structure of Log Buildings; and I had two minutes in the Kitchen before Marie Antoinette's Love Fuss.

Gram's Kitchen Stove was odd, but enough like the one on Jackson Hill to be positively A Stove. The Furniture and the contrasting Color of Vermillion Paint and Lime Wash and the Muzzle Loading Guns that hung on the Topsides of the Round Log Joist under the Ceiling Panels were all as strange as imaginary ornaments from The Moon. But they were materialized Subjects at Hand and I wanted to take inventory.

And Peter Rondeau had estranged Himself to me so that He was stronger than Marie Antoinette and He had greatly bewildered me. So, wishing to ponder, I seated myself on The Fringed Lap Robe absolutely innocent of the contents of the Pine Chest that was under me. I was a six year old Boy. I wanted to please, but it was difficult to know before hand what would please and what would not. And at times things would come up that I could not make myself like.

The conclusion on the Lap Robe was as follows: I would have gotten along passively well alone with Gram and, after skipping some questions, I might have answered a few and She would not have asked so many if it had not been for Peter Rondeau. And His "Can't you talk?" gave me another person to consider when I could hardly talk, and made it positive that I could not talk. And in the last of His Dash I did not want to talk. And the faze of His part that estranged me most was His Strange new tone of voice.

I had never seen Peter Rondeau away from Home; and at Home He only had two tunes—when he was mad and when he was not. And His "The Cats have eaten His Tongue," I could not work to any conclusion, so I gave up that part and presumely left it to the cats. Then I got an Idea, just temporary, in Mental Embryo, and subject to change: Nevertheless a surmise: That Peter Rondeau had a Special Reserve of Cute Sayings for Special Occasions away from Home when He had shaved with His Monstrosity Wade & Dutcher Razor and Polished His Fine Boots with Bixby's Boot Black.

Then Aunt Delia Corrow, in Her Teens and the Baby of the Family, came along and she sat on the Lap Robe to have a Talk with Me. She had a lot of Laughter and all I remember of that Talk she informed me: "We are sitting on The Wedding Cake to give it a bad taste." And She went away laughing.

Exploring Grandma's House

After she departed I walked about the Room. The Side Walls were the Great Big Logs of The Main Construction and they were done with Lime Wash as White as the Mystic Loaves on the Fence Posts. And the Ceiling was very low, enough so that a Tall Man had to Salute slightly as He went under the largest Floor Joist over Head. And the Joist and Panels between them were all neatly papered.

And the East Wall had a Doorway that went through two thicknesses of Big Logs where the two Houses articulated together. And the Door Way was low and broad and cased with boards and papered; And in order to encase the two walls of Big Logs the casing was about four feet wide; So that going through that Door Way was rather like going through a Short section of Hall Way.

Each house had a board petition for the four Rooms of the Double House. The two outer End Rooms were Kitchens, and the two Middle Rooms were used as Living Rooms or Bed Rooms. And at previous times two Families had lived there.

And as I made my first temporary visual survey of the Northerly Living Room, there were many wonderful and interesting things; And I remember three Pictures that hung on the Wall. They were in Colors, and Neatly

Framed, and two of them were large size. One was known as "Rose Bud," a stylish well dressed pretty Maiden Lady with a large becoming Hat ornamented with Ostrich Feathers, and She had a Parasol with Glittering Fringe in Her Hand. And according to the time She was laced to Neck Size at the Waist. The Picture was not a Unique Antique Painting. It was available unframed for twenty-five "Lantz Brothers Soap Wrappers" that had a picture of an Etopian, and it came on a Bar of Brown Laundry Soap.

Another Picture was "A Live Size Blue Jay on a short section of Pine Limb" and even the Pine Needles looked very real, and all were in appropriate colors. The other Picture was of smaller size. It was of "Pope Leo X" Dressed in Red and with Beads and Cross; And a small Skull Cap on His Head.

I was not in anyway done with that Room, but I went to the Kitchen. Three of the Perpendicular Walls were the Big Logs and they too had their semi-annual White Wash for over forty years. The Lime was thick on the Old Logs and made them whiter than Snow. The Walls were so white that Two Windows, about a yard square, lighted The Kitchen like out-of-doors.

The Open Stair Way of Smooth Boards, The Low Broad Doors and Casings and a Sink were all Painted Vermilion to French Taste. And the Vivid Vermilion made a striking contrast against The Perfect White of The Walls. The Low Ceiling was like that in The Living Room only it was done with Yellow Oaker. Half a dozen Muzzle Loading Guns of varied types and calibers hung in Leather Loops on the sides of the Round Joist Timbers overhead. And in one corner there was a Large Two Door Cupboard that was painted Blue. And in the Middle of the North Wall, one of The Broad Doors opened into the Outside Cellar.

Then as I was taking The Kitchen's Setting, Hubert Geror came in with Two Rabbits; He had been out in

The Rabbit Swamp near by, tending His Copper Wire Rabbit Snares. And He put The Two Rabbits on the rank of Stove Wood back of The Kitchen Stove. Then I stood for several minutes looking at my first rabbits. They were nearly as White as Gram's Walls; And one had Fresh Blood on His Nose and one still had The Copper Wire Snare on His Neck. And Hubert Geror's Rabbits were perfectly Legal, even caught in Copper Wire Snares, Jan. 1st, 1890.

The Conservation (So called) Commission of New York State was not born at that time, except that shortly before 1890, Governor Hill had appointed Four Men as a Conservation Measure in New York State. And its a Sure Guess that even The News of that appointment never reached The Log House. And it had Not Thought to make a Law to direct Hubert Geror's foot steps when He carried a Varying Hare.

In fact it took many years after 1890 for the Conservation Commission of New York State to reach The High Point of American Lowness, waste, dishonesty, degeneracy and hateful dictorship. To fine Charles Corrow's Neighbor, Henry Mitchel—twenty five dollars for killing a Bear in His Own Pasture; After the Bear had killed, ruined and wasted a Cow and a Calf that belonged to The Same Henry Mitchel.

And it took about as long for The Same Caliber of Conservation (Conservation?) to Arrest The Writer repeatedly on Frame Up Malignant Charges, and cart to Jail, hold for twenty-four days at a time, starve, fill full of Lice and Bed Bugs. And The Conservation Commission having had some uncomplimentary exposure in the twenty four days and not getting an Indictment, They left it to H. W. Main to "Let Me Go."

That's all the redress I got. And at that time "The Conservation of New York State" took Twenty Five Dollars worth of Fur and a Deer Skin away from me; and a year later They Arrested me again.

They said "We want to clean this up." They made a kind of Kangaroo Court for me at Saranac Lake. But I observed there was nothing clean about it, so I demanded a Jury Trial and later I went with a Witness and pled my own case. They brought in the Deer Skin which never was worth Three Dollars and which They had Mildewed so it was quite worthless. I took The Deer Skin away from Their Crooked American Hands. To me it was no Great Victory; People complimented me, but as usual much of that was The Usual Bologna.

It was like this: The Deer Skin cost me less than Three Dollars and now after nineteen Months in Ray L. Burmaster's care at Saranac Lake it was not worth a Dollar And it cost me Twenty Dollars to make the repeated journeys to Saranac Lake.

Not that I wanted The Deer Skin at Twenty Dollars, but it was that under the circumstances, or Plead Guilty when I was not guilty and pay An American Tiny Wee Bit of a fine to the American Conservation Commission. The twenty five Dollar Fur was taken the same time The Deer Skin was taken; And it was taken to The Kangaroo Court: Perhaps to help scare a Fine. But it refused to be brought in before The Jury Trial—Though I was under arrest for it. And just a little further: It never was returned.

It was done by American Officials under a pretense "Of Law." But it was absolutely False and Malignant and it has no more Ground of Honor than the Lowest Chicken Thief that ever robbed a Chicken Roost or The Lowest Gangster that ever Robbed a Bank. This is only a pass: There is no space here to do justice to The Subject "Conservation Commission." Suffice to say—In the Nineties Geror's Rabbits were legal and Henry Mitchel would not have been fined at that time for killing a Wild Bear that came in The Pasture and killed a Good Cow.

Grandpa and Grandma Corrow

According to a bit of History I learned later: Charles Corrow and His Marie Antoinette (Nee Larmey) were born in Canada. They married there rather young and they came to New York State before they begat Children. And they settled in the Log House where they lived about half a century. Their Eight Children were born there and all but one who remained a Bachelor, Married and launched from there.

Charles Corrow, very early in Life, had experience on the Ocean as a Sailor. And later he had about three years in the Civil War. He had been in many Ports and in many Battles. And in spite of the fact that he had no schooling he was rather an interesting Man to visit with. Judging from what the Scribbler remembers of him during the Nineties, when Charles was in his Sixties, he must have been quite an able man physically when in his Prime. Even when well along in the sixties he used to like to take hold and twist Wrists with the Men of the time. And he liked to Jig Dance and he liked his Toddy a bit.

He had a unique patriotism of his own style without any thought of the usual formalism of the subject, and he used to parade about Ausable Forks in his Blue Uniform. And on Decoration Day he marched with the Veterans to the Cemetery where they put flags on the graves of comrades whom they had known in the Civil War, and later as Neighbors and Friends about Ausable Forks and Palmer Hill.

When he was seventy-four I remember him marching on the streets of Plattsburgh for several hours one evening in the Autumn of 1900. He carried a kerosene torch and he laughed and nodded his head approvingly every time the marchers shouted for William McKinley.

For many years before the nineties the J. & J. Rogers Company of Ausable Forks was engaged in the Iron Industry. The final aim was to produce Pig Iron for shipment at Point of Rock Station near the Ausable River, three miles below the village of Ausable Forks. And the Ready Iron at the Station represented much labor back of it in many branches.

First was the mining of the Raw Iron from the Inner Strata of Palmer Hill and Jackson Hill; At that time the drilling was done by hand with Churn Drills and Striking Hammers. And the blasting to break the Raw Iron was done with black powder. Then the Iron was hoisted to the surface and then it was hauled by Horses over Planked Roads to Crushers where it was crushed and separated from the rock material. Then the pure iron, in coarse gravel form, was hauled farther to Forges where Bloomers processed it with their Char Coal Fires and hammered it into chunks they called Pig Iron.

There were many auxiliary works and perhaps the most expedient was producing Char Coal.

There were many men throughout the Woods for a radius of five or six miles from the Forges. They built log houses and log shanties and in time acquired a clearing and gardens and many other things for themselves. They paid no rent. The Rogers Company owned the Land and it was considered as very congenial by all involved. And the men's work for the Rogers Co., was chopping Kiln Wood and building Brick Kilns and making Earth Pits and producing Char Coal and hauling it to the Forges to perpetuate the Bloomers' Fires to process the Iron.

Accordingly Charles Corrow worked for the Rogers Co. for many years and he acquired clearings and log buildings and cattle and fruit trees and a score of other things that gave him all the privilege of a semi-farmer except paying taxes. And many years before I was born he had about ten men come from Canada and chop wood for him all winter. Perhaps they built a shanty to facilitate lodging accommodations. And as a result two of the Canadian Choppers stayed with Gramp Corrow and made it their home at the Log House for about the rest of their years. And they were Peter Pudvan and Hubert Geror.

Peter Pudvan was born about 1820; he had married and his wife was dead and he had at least a son in Canada. And Peter went to Canada for the winter. But in early spring about the time the Robins arrived, Peter returned to Charles Corrow and stayed until late Autumn for many years.

And as Peter journeyed from the Log House in New York State and Canada and back while the Corrow Girls were Children, he brought several dolls from Canada and he brought them one at a time to present to a Little Girl at the Log House. At that time Dolls were scarce that were two foot tall and walked and cried and went to sleep and woke up and said "Momma." And besides, Shekiels were scarce too. It was many years after that time when the price for chopping four foot Wood went up to the great height of fifty cents per Cord.

The Dolls from Canada came in five pieces of earthen. They were well made and glazed in pure white and pretty. And the five pieces were a small Handfull. And after they arrived at the Log House the Little Girl and Marie Antoinette got the Sewing Box and Remnants of Cloth, and they made a Doll's Body to which they articulated the five pieces of earthen. And then they took fine white cloth fabric with design in color and they made a doll's dress and a narrow ribbon in color made a sash. And in some cases they made a pair of Stockings an inch long.

Thus the Baby Doll was born and it was a Pretty Little Lady but not over six inches tall. The Lips were red, the Cheeks were pink and the Eyes were black and the representation of Hair was blackish color.

The Bachelor Hermit Scribbler having loved children and having bought dolls in the twentieth century can easily imagine the joy of the Little Denizen of the Woods in the Log House when she got her Little Doll.

In time The Little Girl was a Young Lady and she wanted to put the Doll away, but not far away: she wanted to take up Finer Slippers and Fan and Parasol. So she got Card Board, Needle and Thread and Paper and Adhesive and she made a Niche: A Box the size of an ordinary Cigar Box but shorter. Then the Doll was installed and fastened to the Bottom of the Box. Then a Wreathe was made of Little Roses and Fringe of Tissue Paper in variety of Colors. And when the Wreathe was installed it passed over the Doll's Head and down along each side to about her Little Feet. Then a Glass was put over the Box and Paper and Cloth and adhesive secured the edge of the Glass to the edge of the box neatly. And a Loop of Cloth was put on the Box with which to hang it. Then the niche was hung on The Old Log Wall.

On the Day of Aunt Maggie's Wedding, when the Living Room and Kitchen proved a Museum to me, there were three such Niches hanging on the Wall of the Living Room and one of them was Maggie's, who was a Bride that day.

Hubert Geror

Hubert Geror was vastly different from Peter Pudvan charectly, and he was several years younger, of medium stature and for a Canadian Frenchman, rather light. He never married, never went to School or learned a Trade; but he was a very handy workman and neat and orderly and he was modest and mild. And even if it was somewhat dormant, he must have had a love for the Old Log House and the Clearing and its Surrounding Hills. For thirty or forty years he seldom went out of their radius. Once in a few years he went four miles to the village of Ausable Forks and while there he stayed with one of the Corrows who had married and settled there.

He built a little Log Stable and he kept a small flock of sheep. He took good care of them and each Sheep was a Long Wool White Sheep that looked like a Prize Winner.

Hubert Geror was a good Wood Chopper, a good Butcher, and he could apply himself to all labor requirement of that time. He could build a Cup Board in the Wall, put up a Stone Wall or Brick Chimney to quite a degree of perfection. When it came to raising a square of logs for the Body of a Building he had the practical philosophy of notching and fitting the Logs so that the corners fitted together like a cute puzzle.

In that day phonegraphs and Radios had not yet come to Spoil People. People's personal singing had not been muted by Records by Leon Spencer and Gilbert Jerome. And they did not buy Radios and Batteries and pretend to be entertained by anything like the later outstanding program for repetition of "Brush Your Teeth Twice a Day, and see Your Dentist twice a year." Even when compulsory, such a program should be accepted only as a License and Absolution for cursing, without farther Penance than having listened to such a program even when wedged between two verses of song by a Modern Homosapian American Screech Owl of the twentieth century.

This is only a ninety-nine percent criticism for the Radio Screech Owl and it could be much more favorable if it was not for the Overdone Nervewrecking Imposition of the Advertisement. I know I like to hear Kate Smith but even Kate with her good voice is not worth tending radio and tolerating the necessary multiplicity of advertisements and Screech Owls in order to get Kate under the circumstances.

Having said this much about Radio Screech Owls, the best I can do is to apologize to the first feathered Screech Owl I meet in the Woods. However, in the nineties when a dozen people gathered in a Log House for an evening, the majority sung their song and where there was an Old Fiddle in tune many took part at Jig Dancing.

Hubert Geror lived natural and he was a very good Singer. And his song was never cut in two to make a recess in the middle to induct anything like "Alka Seltzer" or a "Best Soap." His song didn't need that anymore than it needed "Worm Cure" or "A Democrat's Old Political Gold-Brick" under the name "New Deal." And all that such a twisted practice could have done then is what it's doing now: Fool most people, rob all of Them, spoil the song and play dishonestly on people's Nerves as an imposition against their wishes.

Geror had a Shot Gun and His Rabbit Snares and he had a Garden. He had a generous size Pine Wood Box in which he kept a supply of Smoking Tobacco and Punk and Flint, and in time, Matches. And two or three cured and dried Pig Bladders to make future Tobacco Bags. And he was the proud possessor of one of the Pine Chests. And he positively made the best shaped and most practical White Oak Axe Helves that I ever saw.

It seems quite positive that his good balance and good judgement carried him through his sixty-six years of life with a full measure of contentment and with very little cash or trouble. And early in the twentieth century he died at the house of one of the Corrow Girls, who had married and had her Home in the Village of Ausable Forks.

And it is because of lack of space and with repugnance that a brief can't be given here on how Peter Pudvan and Hubert Geror lived at the Log House for over thirty years and how impossible it would be today according to the change of trend.

Jig-Dancing Exhibition

The Hands of the Clock kept moving as before, and after, and about ten o'clock the two Hanks came along with The Prancing Horses. They were after The Bride: and they tied the Horses to Posts near the Outside Cellar and they came in the Kitchen. There was Cheer and Talking and Laughing and Good Humor.

The Bridegroom went in the Living Room and talked with the Bride for a minute and then he went back in the Kitchen.

The Miners peeled off their Over Coats, but they hardly took Chairs; they went to Gramp with a few words and then to Gram and then to Mr. Geror and then around again. The Gab Feast was on. The Seniors, Corrows and Miners had known each other since before The Bridal Couple were born. And Hank Sr. and Grandpa Charles used to nag each other with their French jokes.

They were Jig Dancers who could take a part according to the day, but usually they had to be coaxed or urged on a bit in some way. And so Charles accused Hank of "Beating Him" even "By cheating" the last time he Played Cards with him. And Hank told Charles "I never cheat: You can't play cards as good as I can, that's why you can't win." And further: "If I can come back this evening I'll beat you Jig Dancing."

Perhaps others were urging for a dance. The first thing I knew Charles Corrow sprang from His Chair and as he went toward Henry Miner he gave Hank to understand "You have been boasting long enough, and when it comes to Jig Dancing, I can take the conceit out of you now and not wait until Evening." And the two Old Daddys began to Jig Dance in the middle of the Kitchen.

The Bride was in the Living Room with Her Sister adjusting Her Veil, and she came to the Door with Her Veil in Her Hand and she watched the Dance. The Two Old Gaffers Danced like Fighting Mad for five minutes and when it came to a close it was a Scream for everyone. Hank was about in his Fifties. He was Short and very Stout and he had a Cropped Little Reddish Mustache. Grandpa Corrow looked like a Tall Santa Claus with a bulk of White Whiskers.

Such a Spirit especially early in a program always infuses better Humor in Good Humor. I had never seen anything like it, in fact I had not known that people Jig

Danced; and it would not have been more strange if two men of peculiar type with their eyes in the back of their heads had arrived from Mars, riding backwards on Bicycles and stopped to give a Martian Stunt. I was not watching to see who was the Best Dancer in order to make myself A Hero Worshipper: I had no authority and no thoughts as to comparison. It was more like a first peek and see at a New World. The commotion of the Dance and the Tune played on the Floor by the Shoes held me positively. It was my first Jig Dance. And in after years I never saw any better in a Specialty in Vaudeville Shows, and I never saw an Old Warpy Floor get a better spanking from two Old Pairs of Shoes.

In a few moments the Bride was attired with Her Trousseau and she came into the Kitchen; she kissed Mother and Daddy Good Bye, and they were on their way.

We all followed them out of the Old Log House and to the Ornamented Garden Gate. And the two Hanks loosed the Horses from the Posts within fifty feet from the Garden Gate. The Air was still winter sharp but the Sun had taken possession of the Day and it was Cheerfully Nice. The Bridal Couple got into their Cutter and Henry Sr., got into His Cutter, and they Tucked Their Winter Lap Robes about them and they Commanded the Horses.

The Horses had stood in the Winter Atmosphere for fifteen minutes and they wanted to go, so much so that the first start off was a Slow Moving Prance. The Bride waved to Mother and Mother waved back to Maggie. Perhaps that's what got my attention and I looked up at Gram: Her Glasses were pushed back on Her Forehead to the Edge of her Blanching Hair and her Eyes were Flooding and I did not know but the Flood would Over Flow. But no, Marie Antoinette was brave.

I hurried back in the Kitchen to watch through the Little Window and see them go; they soon disappeared back of the Little Log Stables. And they made the Curve on the Road and then they reappeared past the Stables. It was a pretty sight but it only lasted half a minute; the Tassels on the Horses' Heads and the Bride's Ribbons floated on the Winter Air; the prancing of the Horses was over and they were stretching out and making good speed and in a Few Seconds they disappeared among the Oaks and the Clumps of Cats.

Then for several hours at midday we were left to socialize at the Log House; and for an Hour Gram was quite silent; not that she had any sorrow or that she would have it any different, but her many remembrances of much personal experience and the Beauty of the occasion had touched her. And with all the gratifying situations and the joy of the Day, there was this fact for Gram: Lovable Maggie was going.

Maggie never lived over five miles away from the Old Folks, and there was nothing regrettable about Hank and Maggie as the years proved; and Gram's Internal Touch was rather a Joyous One and the noticeable faze accordingly was rather a revelation of her Good Qualities and Tenderness as many an Old Blanching Mother has felt.

Further Exploration and Observation

I had made at least a round in the Kitchen and Living Room and I knew that I had a Very Large Stock to investigate. So I made a round about every hour. And every time I found something new and each time around I looked out through all the Little Windows and I made a Mental Semi-tictious Survey of the Clearing and the Little Stables. And I seem to know that something awaited me outside but I was too young and winter snow and cold was too severe for me to be permitted to investigate Out Doors.

Besides I was in no state of efficiency to survey a Clearing so far from Home. I had left my Cardinal

Points on Jackson Hill; and here "Up Hill" and "Down Hill" were comparatively topsyturvy and John Breen and Billy Peckham were I know not where and they were of no use to me as points of reference until I went back around the Mountains to the Old Dewyer House on Jackson Hill.

And as I learned in the immediate years that followed, Gramp's Clearing and the one on Jackson Hill would compare roughly: The Clearing itself, the heaps of Cobble Stones, the Apple Trees and the Annual, BiAnnual and Perennial Plants all compared. Of course everything and its setting was different to the last Apple Tree and Pine Stump. And there were many new strange things too. But the great dissimilarity were the Buildings and their contents.

During the day as I looked many times through the Little Kitchen Windows, I saw Cattle and Sheep out of doors, eating Hay and walking about the Stable Yard. And a Spotted Cat slunk along the Snow Trail. And Grandpa came out of the Stable and came to the House with a Fiber Pail in His Hand.

Again I stood with my Hands in my Pockets and looked over the Rabbits for a while; then I discovered that the Stairs did not exactly reach to the Kitchen Floor, but there was a Flat Form over a yard square that elevated about seven inches above the Floor and the Stairs were set on top of the Flat Form. Furthermore one side of the Elevation was open and afforded a Cubby under the Stairs. And in the Cubby there was a Boot Jack.

I brought out the Boot Jack and I sat on a Chair near the Sink and for a while I made a thorough examination of the Boot Jack. It was only a Forked Stick with a Little Stick nailed crosswise under the Main Stick to hold it in proper position when in use to pull off a boot. But it was old and much used and the years and wear had browned and polished it so it proved a curiosity and I put it back in the Cubby only to bring it out again several times during the day.

Again I went in the Living Room and I stood and glanced at my Picture Gallery—"Rose Bud"—"Blue Jay" and "Pope Leo." Then I stood before a Niche that hung on the Wall and I made a careful Visual Survey of the Little Doll. Then I moved to the next and the next and so I made the Stations of the Dolls.

And after the session with the Dolls I looked about the Room and I discovered a Photograph Album on a Stand. The Album was large and it had a Green Plush Cover that was padded so the cover was very thick and it had a broad Ornamented Bronze Clasp. So I looked at it for a while and it was all strange and for all I knew it might prove to be a Box Full of Assorted Buttons or it might be Hubert Geror's Smoking Kit with Punk and Flint.

My First Picture Show

In time I dared to touch it and nothing happened. Even the Dolls on the Wall Kept Mum. So I pulled the Album to the Edge of the Stand and I rubbed my Hands on the Velvety Plush and I admired the Glittering Metal of the Clasp. It took a little time but the Clasp opened and I lifted the Thick Cover and I turned about two of the Leaves; they were nearly a quarter of an inch thick and on each side of the Leaf there were a half dozen Tin Type Photos. Without knowing Gold I had discovered better than a Gold Vein; so I closed the Book and I took it in my Arms and I went to the Lap Robe.

It was indeed a Luxurious Setting: Near the Pine Chest there was a Little Window with Geraniums and through the Window I could see Fat Bovine and Snow Covered Little Quaint Stables and Broad Snow Fields bordered by the Woods. And I was under a Very Low Ceiling and semi-surrounded by Little Sweet Dolls that stood in Artistic Niche that hung on luring White Walls.

About that time, Hank and Maggie were at the

Church with their Friends from the Village, who came to see them and to express Greetings and congratulations.

For a long time I turned the Leaves of the Photo Album; I had perfect interest almost without being aware of it; and I drank visually with unmolested enthusiasm. I had no worrisome thought about a Smashed Automobile by the Road Side and not even a wondering thought as to what Benjamin Harrison was doing.

It was My First Picture Show and some Fazes of it the future never excelled. And it was the only one ever, Sitting On a Wedding Cake.

I closed the Album with a Child's full measure of satisfaction and appreciation and I put it back on the Stand. And again I was ready to make another Carnival Tour in the Kitchen. And by that time My Rabbits had disappeared: Mr. Geror had taken care of them and he had put them away elsewhere. And Gram was preparing the Midday Meal. She had a Roast of Fresh Pork into which she had jabbed a hundred times with the Point of a Butcher Knife and she had inserted so many small pieces of Garlic and it was roasting in the Upright Oven of the Old No. 9 Plattsburgh Stove.

And she had about Three Iron Caldrons of various Types and Sizes on the Stove and in one of the Caldron she had a Choice Piece of Fat Beef, to which she added Onion and Cinnamon. And as the Caldrons began to boil, the Seasoning and the Juice of Rare Meat diffused a Captivating Odor that filled the Kitchen. And it was then the Two Cats left the Zinc and followed Gram all over the Kitchen crying and coaxing, like Children in quest of Candy.

Many such casual incidents impressed themselves indellibly in my mind and remained as an Open Book throughout many years. And it was about twenty-five years later, I was a Hermit Trapper among the Major Adirondack Mountains and I made a livelihood accordingly for Long Winters during many years. And Fur Animals were Wild and Scarce and for a short period the Market Prices seemed to be more favorable than they had been and it was always desirable to learn anything that would prove of advantage.

I understood Trapping and Wild Animals very well; and I also had something to learn. Then too I had a surmise before, but finally the surmise became serious: that what made Cats Cry especially might appeal to some Wild Animals. I didn't get the Best of Beef and I varied the receipt; and I made a can of bait and I tried it and it worked. But anything might seem to work once. In fact once in a while a Wild Animal can be caught without any Bait, but generally not to any practical advantage. I studied the Receipt parallel with the philosophy I had pertaining to Wild Animals; and I added a few ingredients and thanks to Marie Antoinette—her caldron Flavor and Crying Cats—for over twenty five years it has positively proven to be the Best General Lure that I ever used as a trapper.

And as Gram was setting the Table I viewed the Dishes in the Blue Cupboard and she brought out a little Porcelain Dish and as she showed it to us she said "That was my Gram's many years ago."

Up to that time, that was the most interesting day of My Life. And even then little did I know about all the Visits and Experiences and Happy Hours I was to have at Gram's Log House as a growing Boy all through the Nineties: Inspecting every Nook and Curiosity at House and Stables and surveying the Clearing and Chasing Rabbits in the Swamp. And Prospecting Boy Fashion on the Near By Hills and coming back with a Red Maple Leaf in my Hat and my boyish pockets full of Acorns; and to tell Gram what I had seen.

About Two o'clock the Happy Groom and Bride returned. They had been at the Church and also had called on the Senior Miner Family.

I continued to make my rounds and by that time I had checked my Overwhelming Stock to a standard so I was not making many new discoveries, but it was nevertheless interesting. The Photograph Album and the Dolls proved most captivating and lasted at least all through the Nineties. In fact at least one of the Dolls is still well Preserved in Her Niche.

As I write this line on Feb. 5, 1944 I can't give the Hour with exactness because I have not a Time Recording Piece. And I do not want one except the Sun and Moon and Stars. Accordingly it is nearly Mid Day and the Moon is well advanced as a Waxer. And I'm in a Hermit Trapper's Hut Eighteen Miles from Civilization; and I am sitting on a bear skin that I tanned and I am warming my feet by a Stove that I made with an Oil Drum many years ago.

Half of a Ten Point Deer hangs in a Wigwam near the Huts. The Two Huts' Front Gabels are Ornamented with Deer Horns and Bear Bones. Chickadee Birds come several times per day and pick on a Raccoon Carcass that hangs on the Hut.

I have not seen a Post Office or even a Road in over nine months.

It happens that less than two years ago I called on Aunt Maggie Miner: Uncle Hank had been Laid Away a Year or so and Aunt Maggie was Blanched to Snow White. She was nearly Seventy Six years old and well preserved.

And Her Slightly Blanching Daughter and her Grand-Son and her Great Grand Daughter were with her. The Great Grand Daughter was a Little Tot, and I treated her to Candy and a Ride on my Foot; and I had a Splendid Visit with the Four Generations. I spoke about the Wedding of fifty two years ago. And I seem to remember many Points in detail more vividly than Aunt Maggie did. And as I mentioned, including the Name of the Fiddler, she remembered and seemed to be affected pleasantly. And when I mentioned "The Dolls" she smiled and went away. In a moment she came back with the Niche and the Doll that were hers which Peter Pudvan brought from Canada many years before her Wedding Day. And she showed me the Little Doll, the same representation of Hand Work and in the same state of preservation as I saw it on the Log Wall on the First Day that followed the Gay Eighties.

Well, the Wedding Day advanced and the First Sun of the Nineties was sinking in the West and much to the South of the Ecliptic. Several Relatives and Close Friends arrived with More Jangling Bells and Prancing Steeds. The Steeds (Auto Engines of the Day) were stalled in the Log Stables (Garages of the Day) with Hay for Gasoline and Grain to Charge their Batteries, and the Folks went in Fine Boots and Winter Togs to congratulate and partake of Supper and Night Dance.

The Wedding Party

When the shades of night had settled over The Winter Hills and Valleys so that the Stables were distinguishable through the Kitchen Window only by their Snow Capped Roofs, the Table was lengthened generously and set; then a Load of Food that made the Table groan for mercy was brought on. And a Row of People was seated on Each Side of the Table, as long as the Kitchen was broad between White Walls. And the Pine Chest yielded the Wedding Cake.

Then Sid Benway came in with his Fiddle Box. The arrival of Sid Benway was anticipated and to see him and hear his Voice was Joyous to the Dancers, and the Sight of the Fiddle Box was confirming that there was Jazz Music in the Box.

For over an Hour they Feasted and Drank their Wine and Sung their French Songs. Then later there was a resetting for Waitress and Children.

And following was the Dance: a few pieces of Furniture were removed from the Living Room; next Gram's Circular Rugs of Dyed, Braided and Sewed Colorful Fabrics were put elsewhere. And Eight people came on the Floor as Four Couples to Dance a Quadrille. I sat on the Lap Robe on half of the Wedding Cake.

Sid Benway set in a corner of the Living Room and he brought the shiny brown Fiddle out of the Fiddle Box; then he closed the box and he pushed it snug in the Corner. He snapped the Fiddle Strings with his Thumb and that was my first audience to a Violin Sound, and I thought it was pretty cute. Next he rubbed the Bow on a Chunk of Rosin and for all I knew about Rosin at that time, he might have been rubbing the Bow on a piece of Punk or Beef Suet. Next he rubbed the Bow on the Fiddle Strings a bit, and then he hurriedly put the Body of the Fiddle between His Neck and His Knee and with his left Hand he twisted and turned the Pegs and at the same time he worked the Bow across the Strings with his Right Hand and the Fiddle roared and squealed varying discordant groans as if it had an awful, awful Belly Ache.

But Sid Benway soon had the Strings in harmony and the Four Couples were waiting. So Sid stuck the Butt of the Fiddle under his Chin and he began fingering the Fiddle Strings with the Fingers of his Left Hand and at the same time he rubbed and jumped the Bow in skillful play over the Strings. Accordingly he played a variety of Sounds that blended together in lively miraculous musical revelations of wonder. It was far ahead of my Cross Cut Saw that hung near the Window toward John Breen.

And when Sid got going good, some one shouted and the Eight Dancers all started at the same time to go somewhere, but they all changed their mind at the same time and all turned to go elsewhere. Again the Shouter shouted and again the Dancers turned: It was as if the House was on Fire and someone screamed! And all tried to get out and in their excitement, couldn't find the door.

And during the Quadrille, every few minutes a Man would start in a Lively Jumping Stunt, and with the Bottom of his Fine Boots he would give the Old Floor a dozen Loud Slaps right on time with Sid's Fiddle. They danced all night and they had an outstanding Good Time.

Nearly every one present was a Relative of mine, but I had never seen them or any one like them before. They were as strange as if they came from a Planet from an Outer Solar System.

There were minute recesses between Quadrilles and between Changes and Breakdowns and about twice during the night there was a ten minute recess for Quadrille Dancers, while the Floor was given to Jig Dancers. It was a very Royal Celebration of New Year and a Beautiful Wedding which had so many Special Points of Maximum Idealism that as a whole it made the occasion a Homogenous Carnival according to French Log House Custom.

There were Big, Stout, Brunette French Women in Middle Life and some had Arms as big as Swill Pails and their Ears were like Warped Slabs of Home Cured Bacon and on the Ear hung a System of Four Rings. And the first Ring was very small, a mere Wire Ring that went through the Ear. And the Second Ring was an inch in diameter: the upper half was wire size; the lower half was a Flat Metal Gold Plated Crescent Moon with Blackish Inlays. And the two Lower Rings were the same in Type but of much smaller size. And the Four Ring System made a Glittering Dangle that hung from the Slab of Bacon half way to the Shoulder.

And Feminine Heads were not Bobbed until about twenty five years later; and they had their Big Twists of Black Hair done up seeming like Preened Black Pullets on top of their Heads.

And at that time Skirts had not been abbreviated at the other End; they were lined and like Jackson Hill

Stairs they Reached from the floor to the Top of the First Story. The scent of various Perfumes filled the Room; and one might surmise that they were a Semi-Disguised Cast of Characters, Representing the Court of Saint Lewis.

My Aunt Delia and Aunt Julia were yet in their teens; and there were Young Men trying the Stunt called "Buzzing." I did not know what it was all about but in after years, according to my advancing Experiences and Practice, I decyphered their Code.

And about four Hours after the Beginning of the Dance, Mid Night Luncheon was served and they Whittled the Wedding Cake to a Mere Remnant which was put back in the Chest. The Dance was resumed and I went back on My Throne; and not knowing the direction towards John Breen and Billy Peckham, I watched toward Sid Benway and the Fiddle and the Dance.

The Good Time kept up at its High Gleeful Standard of Enthusiasm and finally they formed on for the Last Quadrille and the Dance started about as usual. And I looked through the Little Window and Morning Dawn was fast Eliminating the Darkness of Night and taking possession to make another Day. The Little Stables were as plain as Billy Peckham's Roof had appeared twenty four hours before. I was tired and very sleepy. It was only the Luring Appeal of the Dance and the Fiddle and the strangeness and newness of all the people and their doing accordingly that kept me up all night after such a Big Day.

Presumely the Last Dance came to its close Serenely and Satisfactorily, and according to its time and place was as appropriate as the first dance of the Evening. But I have no further authority.

It was at least twenty five hours since I had been taken out of Bed on Jackson Hill. And before the end of the Last Dance, what was left of me went to sleep on what was left of the Wedding Cake.

Two Years Later — Iron Mines and Mining

New Year's Day in 1892 was vastly different in experience and spirit to the Wedding at the Log House two years previous. The winter of 1892 was unfortunate for many of the people of Palmer Hill and Jackson Hill and especially for the local workers in Iron Mines on Arnold Hill.

Since the Wedding at the Log House, the Iron Industry had closed at Palmer Hill and Ausable Forks, and accordingly many of the laborers moved elsewhere. But Peter Rondeau remained at the Dewyer House on Jackson Hill and he found work in Iron Mines on Arnold Hill.

And one—Will Nolan—remained in his little home on Palmer Hill and he too found labor on Arnold Hill. But it was a three mile walk for Peter Rondeau morning and night; and at least four miles for Will Nolan.

There it is: those men worked 60 hours per week; And Peter Rondeau walked at least 36 miles per week; and Will Nolan at least 38 miles each week. And they wore blue overalls and frock and especially in winter—plenty of Fabric under the Blue Vestment. And their Boots were made of heaviest leather—the soles were nearly an inch thick held fast with hard wood pegs and I remember Peter Rondeau bringing home a pair of such new Boots @$4.00—about 1891. He also had two boxes of round head tacks and one by one he put the Boots on a hard wood last he had made and he drove the Tacks in soles and heels until the bottom of the Boots were partly covered with the semi-global tack heads. And so—walking with such Boots on the feet was rather walking on metal instead of leather. And this was necessary to prolong the wear of the Boots! Because, even the coarse leather would not last very long on the rough floor of the drift—which floor was the sharp edges, roughness and distortion of broken Iron Ore and Rock, as left in geological strata after blasting of dynamite deep under the surface in Arnold Hill.

And the Headdress for a Miner was similar to a rain hat, but heavier, and a pit lamp was attached to the hat and when the lamp was fueled, trimmed and lighted it was a flaming torch.

As for Peter Rondeau he had to be up and stirring before 5 a. m. and it's self explanatory that Will Nolan had to part with his bed about 4 o'clock. They ate beans and corn and drank tea of the time; and they took their dinner pails and started out with flaming torch on head gear to cover the miles to the light hole of the Pit where they labored on Arnold Hill. The first start off for Will Nolan was a half mile on a foot trail through the woods and then he came to a main road. But the main road was the rough stony road on Jackson Hill, referred to in a previous chapter, where it took a week at times to check the traffic of one Yoke of Oxen or one team of Horses.

And when Will Nolan had traveled a half mile on Jackson Hill High Way he was approximately going by Billy Peckham's, and another half mile took him to the Dewyer House. And as he approached the Dewyer House he shouted to Peter Rondeau and if Peter Rondeau was not already on his way toward John Breen's he would open the door and shout back to Will Nolan.

The Scribbler of the present lines was very young in later days of 1891 and early days of 1892, but he remembers perfectly well getting up at 5 a.m. on some occasions and sitting near the Kitchen Stove while Peter Rondeau ate his breakfast. And accordingly he remembers Will Nolan coming in the Dewyer House two hours before daylight and sitting on a fifty cent Kitchen Chair near the door, while Peter Rondeau donned a Blue Frock, lit a Pit Lamp, took Mittens and Dinner Pail and the two men were off toward John Breen's. And as they left the Dewyer House they perpetuated for a minute for the scribbler's auditory—the music of their voices as they went talking and laughing as if they were on a Sunshine Picnic. They also perpetuated for a moment the scribbler's optics—the vision of two vivid flames of living fire in the blackness of night. And it seems those men never realized the semi-voluntary and compulsory industrial slavery they were into.

The last mile of the journey to Arnold Hill was another foot path through the woods. As they approached the mine they met men who were the workers from the night shift who were on their way home or to a near by Boarding House. Will Nolan and Peter Rondeau stopped daily at the Engine Room as "Wise Virgins" to get Oil for their Lamps; and in a few minutes they would be on their way down in a Shaft through Strata of Earth to opened drift in Stratum of Iron to do ten hours of hard work getting out Iron.

Accordingly—Peter Rondeau went from the Dewyer House to Arnold Hill to work New Year's Day 1892, and when he reached the Power Room near the opening of the Mine, he found his Comrads and Co-workers in a mental state of gloom and sorrow stricken. The Day Shift was arriving and getting the news from the Night Shift. The news was: As the Night Shift came up out of the mine, one of their numbers was killed in what seemed a heartsickening hard way. For the first morning of 1892 it seemed positive that all the men of the Night Shift except one came up out of the Mine by way of the long ladder system; Man after Man, Torch after Torch, Hand over Hand, Iron Rung after Iron Rung—a thousand Rundle—more or less—according to the depth of the Mine.

And one John Rock chose to ride up the Shaft in the Skip. Generally there was plenty of room in the Shaft, but at one or two points—the Rocky Roof was so low that there was just room enough for the Skip to go through under the Metal Roof. That morning John Rock's Lamp was trimmed and burning and he knew the mine quite well; but he must have forgotten himself and allowed himself to be off his guard at least one second too long. The speedy Skip* going three times as fast as a man would walk caught John Rock against the Roof and instantly cut his head off against the edge of the Skip. Then as the Skip went up to the surface, John Rock's Head went bounding down the Shaft, blacker than Midnight over rails, timbers, trusswork and huge broken chunks of Rock and Pools of Riley Water—as if seeking a level or obstruction where it might stop.

The Skip reached the surface ahead of the men who went up by way of the Ladder and when they got on top of the Earth, they found John Rock's Body in the Skip but no head, so they went a few paces to the Engine House and it was about that time that Peter Rondeau, Will Nolan and others arrived at the Engine Room.

About daylight, some one went to John Rock's Home to tell his Widow and his little children about John's last ride in the Skip. And Peter Rondeau and Will Nolan and others trimmed their lamps and went down in the Mine, not to work as usual but to search for John Rock's Head.

The Hermit Scribbler remembers well the midday hour of that January 1st, when Peter Rondeau came home and reported the disaster of the night—and he added "Up to ten o'clock when I left the Mine, we failed to find the Head." Later in the day John Rock's Head was found and brought to the surface in a pail.

In the two months that followed the death of John Rock several more men were killed in Arnold Hill Mines. The Mines had been in operation for many years and much rock had been broken that had not enough Iron to pay for hoisting, crushing and separating and some of the Rock was hoisted to the Surface and dumped as a bank near the mine to make a riddance of the Lean Rock.

---

*Note—Skip is a metal car with 4 wheels — travels on 2 tracks, controlled by Drum and cable and used chiefly to hoist Iron in a mine.

Timbers were also used in the Mines to make retaining walls on shelves of abandoned Drift and a multiplicity of tons of broken Rock were stalled back of the Timber Wall to save time and expense of hoisting. In time, for a period, the mining Industry ceased to function. Tools and Machinery were hoisted, the work completely ceased and the laborers went elsewhere. And in a short time, every room and cavity of Shaft and Drift were full of water. After some years, work was resumed. The water was pumped out, new Machinery was set up and in time the Iron Industry operated full time for Arnold Hill.

During the aquatic period the timbers water logged and rotted and later as the timbers dried under their heavy load—all was slightly shook by blasting and sometimes a timber would break and let down a few tons of Rock that made the Mine a dreadful place, dangerous to work in and finally, one day in March, more Timbers broke and a Chamber full of broken Rock fell to a lower level and trapped and crushed . . .

Cold River flow upstream from Hermitage.

Noah John on Ampersand Mountain, September, 1924.

The Hermit's City at Cold River.

Noah John at Shattuck Clearing.
c. 1935

Close up of Hall of Records, Cold River City — Note notched logs.

The Frenchman and the Indian N.J.R. and Dan Emmett. Photo by Bill Petty.

The Hermit-Mayor pondering weighty municipal matters.
Photo by Ed Hudowalski.

Left to right: Dr. William Gregory, Mrs. Jay L. Gregory, Mrs. William Gregory and ye Hermit.

Photo of Noey John which won award for Jay L. Gregory in New York HERALD *contest 1929.*

The Hermit, his woodpiles (wigwams), Hall of Records and Town Hall at left.

Hizzoner and his Cold River bailiwick.

Chef Rondeau in action.

Rondeau and part of dinner party at Hermitage.

The Hermit retrieving canned goods from Cold River.
Courtesy of New York State CONSERVATIONIST.

NOAH JOHN RONDEAU
Adirondack Hermit

And there the recollections abruptly end - - smack dab in the middle of a sentence, thus creating what might be termed a minor mystery. Logically, it would seem only natural to assume that Noah would at the least have completed the sentence if not the paragraph. The more obvious concern of course was that the rest of the reminiscences had actually been written but were later lost—or possibly were now in some other person's possession.

Therefore, there was an understandably profound feeling of relief when, in one of Noah John's letters, the explanation was given in the following welcome words: "On my last debut at Cold River I wrote four poems and a manuscript (119 pages) of prose—my Recollections of 60 years ago. It is about a French Wedding in a Log House and when in type it will reduce to about 40 pages. It's an Outstanding Scream!" . . .

However, it is regrettable that the hermit did not continue with this project because by doing so he would have furnished many missing details and vignettes dealing with the rest of his childhood and early manhood as well as relating further particulars about his father's experiences in the Arnold Hill iron mines.

Other than the humiliating experience provoked by his father during the festivities at the time of his Aunt Maggie's marriage, very little is known about Noah's early years.

His journal entries made many years later provide evidence that Peter Rondeau must have been anything but an indulgent, permissive parent. Like all old-time parents he insisted upon strict obedience and would settle for nothing less. Noah, the first born of nine children in the family was apparently somewhat of a maverick—stubborn, hot-headed and rebellious. Even at that age—15—he had already shown impatience with discipline and a love for the freedom offered by the outdoors.

Proof of this comes from four remarks made in the diaries. The first of these, dated Aug. 8, 1963, makes this revealing statement: "65 years ago today (1898) I left Jackson Hill. I ran away from home; left Peter Rondeau[1] his Stick, Abuse of me, his Religion[2], his Priest and his Fool God."

Another entry: "Left Jackson Hill, had dinner at Lewis Bombard's. Sorel mare over Palmer Brook. Night Lodge in Clintonville and breakfast there too. Walk to Port Kent and sleep on Dock. Next day steamboat to Burlington. Walk from Burlington to South Williston." He apparently stayed there with relatives for several weeks; arrangements for doing so had been made by his Aunt Maggie Miner, whom he always considered to be even closer to him than his own Mother.[3]

In another journal appears this savagely caustic comment which he wrote alongside a newspaper clipping entitled "Boy Ten Kills Dad Over Spanking."

Noah's vehement retort was: "Young Paul Sims: I'm glad you shot your Dad. Wish I had shot mine when I was 10—or 5! It would have saved me much Abuse!"

Still another entry shows how deeply Noey resented his father's treatment of him. This particular outburst

---

[1] Noah was the only one in the family who ran away from home. The rest of the children always felt that he never showed proper respect for his parents and that he walked out on his obligations as oldest son.

[2] Peter Rondeau (1856-1920) was a very devout Catholic who worked hard to keep his large family together, first as a miner, later as a blacksmith in Black Brook. At one time when he was too poor to pay his pew rent, the priest would not permit him to sit in one. Determined to attend mass Rondeau made himself a bench and sat at the back of the church. The priest then threw out the bench but Rondeau was not to be denied. He sat on the steps outside the church where he could at least hear the service even though he could not participate.

[3] Alice Corrow Rondeau, Noey's mother, was born in 1858 and died in 1901.

was triggered by an article datelined Portsmouth, Ohio, March 30, 1948: "Wesley Orr, 35, told his son, 'This is going to hurt me more than it will you.' He then began paddling the boy. Shortly afterward the father was taken to the General Hospital for treatment of a dislocated shoulder."

Noah's indignant reply was the following blast — "Yes, Wesley Orr: thirty seconds after paddling your boy, if a Stranger had walked in and seen your son staggering around the room—blind with tears, his little face turning blue because he can't get his Breath and the little Tongue crippling back in the little throat—then Wesley Orr you'd send the Boy to another Room!

"Wesley Orr, you are a Wise man to thrash your little Boy until you dislocated your Shoulder. Too bad it wasn't your Damned Fool Neck!"

The fact that Noah had still not forgiven his Father, even though the latter had been dead since 1920, indicates either festering hatred or uncharacteristic facetious exaggeration—but the odds are heavily in favor of the former.

In 1941, during an interview between the Hermit and the late Billy Burger, writer of "The Adirondacker" column in the Ausable Forks *Record-Post,* Noah supplied many details which help round out our understanding and knowledge of the period which followed his cutting of the home ties: "A person's opinions are the result of his lifetime experience," he observed. "I was a Frenchman and went to school very little and so I was handicapped. I had to learn the English language, which was pretty much like being thrown into a Chinese school. By the time I was 15 I wanted to see with my own eyes and think with my own mind. At that age it was a stern fight but I won. I kept at it and for ten years it was quite a transition. I became absolutely an overcomer . . .

"What I wanted above all was a first class education. From the time I was 15 until I was 33, I sweat for an education and didn't get it, but I got more than the average out of my school days. I went back to grade school, after eleven years, for a term and finished the eighth grade. I barbered at night in Upper Jay and went to school daytime.[1] That was back in 1910 when Halley's comet was parading in view.

"I had to work for a living. The hours were long and the wages small but I learned four trades—barbering, painting, carpentering and mason work. At 33 I checked up and found I wasn't getting along fast enough so, like the poet, I said "What care I?"—and took to the woods."[2]

When Linda Champagne Hart interviewed him at the Lake Placid Hospital during his terminal illness in March 1967, the aged Noey gave her this supplementary information which helps explain his decision to depart toward the tall timber.

"At the time I first went to Cold River, it wasn't premeditation. I was not too well satisfied with the world and its trends. I worked but it was common laborer work at first. In time I had three or four trades but the best pay I could get was $3.00 or $3.50 for ten hours' work. I did a lot of work back then that I could get $20.00 a day for now and for only eight hours. There were even times when I worked ten hours for only $1.50 or $2.00!

"It weren't no good at all and besides I wanted an education. And I done all that hard work and paid board and room—a small price and all that but still there was nuthin' much left over. So-o—I done that all through the '20's. And all the time I wanted a good education. Well,

---

[1] A teacher named Phinney (or Pinney) took a deep interest in Noah, encouraged, assisted, and tutored him as much as possible in his school in Jay. As a result of the winter's instruction, eager Rondeau got the equivalent of a high school education.

[2] Some people in the Saranac Lake - Lake Placid area spread a rumor that N.J.R. went back into the Cold River country to duck the draft in World War I. Since Rondeau was 34 in 1917, the rumor was ill-founded.

that was just about impossible for me under the circumstances.[1]

"And the times too had a lot to do with it. The country was never any good. It was no good then and never will be until it's overthrown. That's the only remedy for a mess like this." Such remarks as these and other outbursts against what he termed Big Fool American Big Business, organized religion, Higher Authority—especially the Conservation Department—the Election, Welfare and Internal Revenue systems all helped create the impression that Rondeau was an agitator and an advocate of revolution if not an outright Communist. In reality he was a short-fused fellow who was only expressing his bewilderment and opposition toward what he felt to be a grossly unjust social and economic establishment. Thoreau, whose books were well known to the Cold River Hermit, was also anything but timid about sounding off loudly and often about similar issues. Moreover, after conceding his intellectual greatness, one can hardly classify Thoreau as an honest-to-gosh hermit since his cabin on Walden Pond was not much more than a mile from Concord, and his mother and sister reportedly delivered baskets of goodies to Henry on almost a weekly basis.

By 1913 or 1914 Noah John had decided that barbering and seasonal odd jobs in the Lake Placid and Saranac Lake areas were not yielding satisfactory results, so he moved his meager stock of possessions to the wilder, more alluring Corey's—Axton section of the Adirondacks. There he found a form of work that was far more

---

[1] In a letter written years later N.J.R. also stated that during the period from 1902-13 he had worked for a short time in a paper mill and in 1904 as bootblack at the Ampersand Hotel on Lower Saranac Lake; also occasionally he worked at the Lake Placid Club as bellman, barber and cottage inspector. There he had met Henry van Hoevenberg. During the winters of 1903-05 he worked as a lumberjack above South Meadows and along several miles of the easterly trail from Adirondack Loj to Marcy. To him the view of the valley and mountains from the Loj to the Cascade turn was as familiar as the Cold River scenery became later on.

appealing to his nature—guiding and trapping! Besides supplementing his earnings as a handyman and caretaker there, his occasional service as second guide introduced him to the remote ponds and streams that feed the Raquette River water-shed. Understandably such a way of life had the same attraction for him that it had for countless thousands of other French-Canadians and made Him—like Them—eager to enjoy the excitement, freedom and adventure offered by constant contention with the wilderness environment.

Indian Dan

Living at Corey's also gave Noah ample opportunity to learn from an expert who was already on the scene. This man, Daniel J. Emmett, better known as Indian Dan, was an Abenaki from a little village on the St. Lawrence River near Sorel, Quebec. Dan, who walked with a limp, was a powerful 220 pound six-footer who featured a thick black mustache which, in spite of his high cheek bones, made him look strangely different from the average Indian, who usually has no facial hair because it is their custom to pull it out. Undoubtedly this distinction was directly traceable to his half-breed father because his mother was a full-blooded Abenaki.

A very resourceful hunter, fisherman and trapper, Dan specialized in the use of snares and poisons and kept the local fox and rabbit population pretty well in check. His trap "sauce," or lure, a concoction compounded of many ingredients, was particularly malodorous but extremely effective and made his tent area rather easy to locate.

The Indian also made superb black ash packbaskets, sweet grass baskets and balsam pillows which found a ready market among the summer residents of the St. Regis-Upper Saranac region. His special forte featured birchbark canoes; among the buyers were Mrs. Post, the Whittums, Avery Rockefeller and a Mr. Sutro of Corey's.

Moreover, he could handle his product with the same

degree of skill. A long-time friend of his recalled that the Indian had beaten him several times, even though the white man used a guideboat over a fairly long course across Upper Saranac Lake. Dan, paddling on one knee in familiar Indian fashion, made the sleek craft fairly leap out of the water at each lunge of the paddle.

Among still other natural Indian talents was his skill in making bows and arrows and in their use. Furthermore, having been apprenticed to a medicine man as a boy, Dan also knew about all there was to know about herbs and their medicinal properties and therefore was able to bring about speedy cures with remarkable success.

Most of Dan's income came from his service as guide for Mrs. Percy Rockefeller, who then rented a large camp on Upper Saranac Lake. She liked Dan and was very generous toward him. At the end of each season Dan went back across the border with more than enough to see him through the interminable Canadian winters. Once, when word reached her that Dan was sick and needed help, she also sent someone to look after him and provided ample funds to do so.

Locally the big Indian had a reputation for being frugal and even somewhat miserly and he carried his money in a dirty deerskin pouch. One of his methods of getting maximum mileage out of his money was by eating out as much as possible. And even though he was supposed to board himself, he showed up frequently when it was mealtime for the outside help at Mrs. Rockefeller's.

Another employee there can still vividly visualize Dan at the breakfast table. Charlie Tyler, the cook, who was famous for his flapjacks, could never quite get accustomed to the Indian's method of disposing of them. While the rest of the men poured maple syrup over the cakes and ate them with a fork, Dan would soak them in bacon grease, fold them over and then mow them away. In the process the pork juice would supersaturate his mustache, drip down his chin onto his belly and thence to the floor. Not exactly as Emily Post or Amy Vanderbilt would recommend but nevertheless an unintentional attention-getter at the table.

Although he was somewhat slovenly at times, Dan could look very presentable when necessary. Whenever he reported for work for his employer, he always wore a clean white shirt and watched his manners. Those who knew him well said that he never drank, swore or smoked and that when he was togged out in his well-fitting Sunday go-to-meeting suit, he was very impressive indeed.

At Indian Carry Chapel, both he and Noah served as ushers for many years.

At that time, before his hermiting days, Noah and Dan were both considered to be very pious and often argued about religion. Dan never did change but Noah's church-going days ended a decade later—after his bitter confrontation with Higher Authority in 1924. Dan, who eventually got too aged and feeble to make the annual trip South died in Canada about 1951. Noah stayed in the region until 1950, when the Big Blowdown caused such havoc that the Conservation Department closed the woods for several years.

In case the foregoing character sketch of Dan Emmett may seem somewhat irrelevant and diversionary, it has been included for two reasons. In the first place it is, so far as is known, the only verbal tribute other than Noah's to the memory of a memorable man. Secondly, it gives Indian Dan the credit for teaching Noah John much of the woodlore which he practiced so effectively later on at the Cold River Flow.

His skill in making packbaskets, bows and arrows, snares and improvised traps[1], his trap sauce (lure), his woodmanship, trapping and hunting techniques—these

[1] Ross Freeman of Corey's, who used to trap with Noah John in the Ampersand Brook region, said that besides blazing trails around his traplines, he used to paint Indian heads or rooster symbols on the trees to serve as guidelines.

came from careful observation and apt appliance of methods which are characteristically Indian in origin—and the Indian had to be Dan.

Further evidence of this training appears in Rondeau's first diary—that for 1932—when frequent references are made to visits and meals with Emmett. One entry states that Noah watched Dan make a birchbark canoe. Another cites his selling 12 balsam pillows for him.

Noah's own tribute to Dan was written in July, 1947: —"At Corey's we stopped for a brief visit with Mr. Dan Emmett. Dan is of French and Indian descent, is 77 years old and for 37 years has had a canvas set up at Corey's, where he makes baskets, balsam pillows and many other useful and ornamental things from ash splints, birch bark and sweet grass. He has limited English and splendid French vocabulary. He is courteous, honest and modest; and he has unique refinement of his own style.

"For 37 years he has enjoyed the utmost respect and confidence of natives and tourists about Upper Saranac Lake and wherever he goes. His friendship and esteem of others is 100 per cent loyal.

"Many have followed him to his remote hunting grounds in the wilds of Canada—and in turn they have taken him to their ranches in southern states and entertained him all winter. And whatever the depth or height, like Madam Curie, he never loses his head. He is 99 per cent worthy and without office or price. He has unchangeable perfect quality." Quite a testimonial!

Among the older residents at Corey's there are many who can still recall with considerable clarity and pleasure both of their colorful and unforgettable summer visitors—Indian Dan and Noah John.

Life and Living at the Hermitage

Noah's first trip to the Cold River country took place in the late fall of 1902, when he hunted and reconnoitered the section for future trapping purposes. His visits thereafter were also seasonal because he did not start wintering there until 1929. His traplines extended from the head of Ouluska Pass, across Cold River and over Couchsachraga (Couchie) to the upper slopes of Panther Mountain.

A man who knew him well during those years was Alphonse Beaudette of Tupper Lake, logging crew foreman for the Santa Clara Lumber Company, who recalls that he had kept Noah supplied with onion sacks filled with dry bread and doughnuts from the camp kitchen well before World War I.

Beaudette also remembers that previous to the building of the Hermitage, Noah had lived in a shack on the bank of Calkins Creek, several miles down Cold River from the Big Dam (built by John J. Anderson of Long Lake), where Noah next settled. The third move took Rondeau to the picturesque spot on the high bluff commanding the superb views of the Flow with the attenuated Santanoni range providing the backdrop and the knobby peak of Couchie dominating the foreground.[1] At this last location, using lumber from the nearby recently abandoned camp of the Santa Clara Company, Noey constructed Cold River City—population one.

This bailiwick consisted of two low-ceilinged cabins —the Town Hall and the Hall of Records—each of which measured roughly eight by ten feet and was covered with canvas and tarpaper held down with rocks, nails and poles. The low-bridge effect, which presented no inconvenience to Noah, who towered all of five-two in his Bean boots, is easily explained. Working alone it is next to impossible for a person to hoist the siding logs any

---

[1] A. T. Shorey of Albany, who knew Rondeau from 1918 until his death in 1967, stated that the hermit's first camp at Cold River was the abandoned blacksmith shop of the Santa Clara Lumber Co. The heating and cooking facility was the big wooden fireplace into which had been installed a piece of stove iron where the flames hit the bottom of the flue. Understandably, the place burned down.

higher; moreover, the lower the roof the easier it is to heat the interior of the domicile and thereby helping solve the persistent problem of avoiding total congealment during the seemingly endless Adirondack winters.

The Town Hall, where Noah slept during the colder weather, was heated by a make-shift but efficient stove made from a fifty gallon oil drum, which the Hermit had scrounged from a burned-out logging camp on the opposite side of the river and trundled home by rolling it along ahead of him. Then by half burying the drum in sand and topping it with a flat section of sheet iron also requisitioned from the same source, the Hermit had an effective do-it-yourself heating plant. Later on he acquired regular stoves.

Another interior feature of the Town Hall was a line of shelves loaded with large glass jars containing salt, flour and grease. Also lining the shelves was a collection of over 60 books, nine of them on Astronomy, others were on philosophy and science. There were also two well-thumbed Bibles and books by Parkman, H. G. Wells and Thoreau. Below the books was a bunk made like a shelf. On this and over a layer of boughs and marsh hay was placed an air mattress, the gift of some visitor; a blanket and then an unusual sheet—a bearskin. His violin case hung from a wire over the bed.

The second structure, the Hall of Records, usually served as a toolhouse and storage space where he hung up his annual supply of winter meat—a buck and a bear. Occasionally, when summer guests arrived, this shack also served as their sleeping quarters.

Undoubtedly, the most notable sight at Cold River City was the semi-circle of wigwams, which usually numbered six or seven. These served a double purpose: as living quarters in the summer and as his winter supply of firewood. Most of the wood-getting chore was done in the early Spring and much of it came from the river in the form of driftwood.

Before erecting his tepees Noah cut his trees nearly through on both sides and at 30 inch lengths. Pre-cutting them this way made feeding the fire an easy matter—all he had to do was give the timber a few quick whacks against the chopping block and the stove was back in business. This resourceful method obviously must have saved the Hermit a lot of worry and labor. In one journal he wrote that during a particularly wicked winter there had been a continuous fire in the stove for 138 days. His longest continuous stay at Cold River was 381 days—from May 1, 1943 to May 16, 1944.

Noey had a very deep and usually subtle sense of humor. For example: Bad years for the nation's economy went scarcely noticed at Cold River. When visitors might comment on the poor financial conditions of the previous season, it would be news to Noah. However, his dry humor was such that he would agree and remark "Yas, it sure wuz a bad year!" or "Hard times, hard times—a slump in the depression (followed by a hearty laugh, then a long silence and a stroking of his beard). His mishandling of words was also characteristic—"I fired my first catridge and hit a big patridge," or when discussing the reproductive rate among rabbits observed "They're so profilic." Flora and fauna became floriae and fauniae.

Other examples of his drollery were the names he selected for his wigwams. One was called the Rotten Wigwam, which was for decayed wood. Another was called Westerly for obvious reasons. A third was the Old Lady, a fourth was the Double Wigwam. Another where he lived and cooked in warm weather was suitably named Mrs. Rondeau's Kitchenette. Still another was called the Beauty Parlor, complete with dry sink (a hollow stump and a bearskull soap dish). The others he called the Trap House and the Pyramid of Giza. Usually he built two tepees a year to replace those he burned for fire wood. These conical structures, which started with a four-pole foundation, were ten to twelve feet in diameter and about twelve feet high.

Inside the Kitchenette bunches and packages of dried herbs and seeds dangled from the twists of bailing wire which held the trees securely together. Smoke from the fire eventually found its way out through the door or between the sloping poles; what smoke stayed acted as a temporary deterrent against the persistent, insatiable insects.

Visitors at the Hermitage were always impressed by the quality and variety of the flowers on which Noah spent endless hours. Some of these were wildflowers which he had found in the woods and transplanted. Others he grew from seeds brought in from outside. Foxgloves, pinks, white daisies and pansies he planted and nurtured in caldrons hung from tripods. In season there was color everywhere in the enclave.

Besides the flowers Noah spent much time trying to coax vegetables to grow in the thin soil. Mostly turnips, potatoes, carrots and squash (beans also had been tried but found irresistible by the countless bunnies and deer which shared the regional lebensraum) helped round out the food supply. Fortunately for Noah this was supplemented during the Spring and Fall by fishermen, hunters and hikers (especially ADK and aspiring 46ers) who came to know Noah well and looked forward with much pleasure to their annual—or oftener—visits with him. Those friends always saw to it that there was a goodly surplus of food to be left behind as a present for the Hermit. But trout, game and wild greens were the main items of his diet during many of the early years at Cold River.

Prior to 1930 he spent only the late Fall and Spring months at the Hermitage but he still had to get in staples such as flour, salt and evaporated milk. These durables sometimes had to be carried in by packbasket some 17 miles or six hours' trail time from Corey's. In later years an obliging caretaker at Ampersand Park or an accommodating Conservation Department employee driving over the truck trail to the Duck Hole would give Noah a lift as far as the Mountain Pond junction of the Northville-Placid trail. Some of his food was brought in by friends via Long Lake and as far as Miller's Falls on lower Cold River. In each area Noah had provided a series of garbage can caches[1] where he could store his food safely and backpack it in the remaining five miles at his convenience.

However, during the first fifteen years—1915 to 1930—practically anything Noah wanted in the line of foodstuff other than what he could forage for had to be hauled in on his back or the backs of his friends.

It is noteworthy also that Bill Petty and some of his Conservation Department colleagues (and for the record it must be said that there were at least several who understood the Hermit and even sympathized with him) frequently air-dropped packages of groceries and other necessities to help tide Noah over the winter. During this period the Latimers, the Gregorys, Dr. Fellows and Dr. Christiernin and the Burguieres among others, also supplied him with food and money from time to time. From 1937 on the Troy and ADK 46ers also helped the Hermit appreciably.

His storage spot for canned food was a shallow section of the Cold River in front of his diggings. For years after he had permanently left this secluded location, there were still a few rusty cans visible in the river.

Noah was also very provident in his method of assuring himself enough food to tide him over when he was hunting or trapping in the remoter reaches of his domain. People who shared his confidence were always somewhat surprised to see him suddenly stop, reach into a hollow

[1] His storage system supplied Noah with this typical remark: "If you ever get tired of home cooking, come back and see Rondeau and he'll give you something good out of the garbage can!"

log or tree and retrieve a jar of coffee, a can of hash or other tinned provender which very likely had originally been stashed there even ten or fifteen years previously.

Such details will help a reader to visualize and identify with Noah in his many years of life and living at Cold River. Even though he did have occasional visitors —mostly hunters, fishermen and lumbermen—during his early tenure days, there was one year (1940) cited in his journals when he had spent all but 10 days alone in his wilderness solitude before trekking out to civilization for his annual Xmas holiday visit with his friend, Frank Hathaway, caretaker of Bartlett's Carry Camp near Upper Saranac Lake. After Frank moved to Lewis, Noah spent several such vacations with Albert Hathaway, caretaker for Pine Point Camp, also at Bartlett's.

Most of the time Noah had no real cause to complain, as he did of Corey's in 1920, that things were getting too crowded and civilized there to suit him. (Shades of Alvah Dunning!) But during the recurrent periods when the level of the liquid in his pots of eternity tea and everlasting stew must have reached dismayingly low points, when he had good reason to be grateful for even an abbreviated meal of old buck and beans, and during frigid winter days when his belly button and his backbone must have established very close contact, one can safely surmise that from time to time, Noah must have often entertained deep doubts about the relative advantages of hermitdom.

Logging Along the Cold River

As has already been noted the earliest year-round occupants of the Cold River region were the loggers employed by the Santa Clara Lumber Company. Twenty years previously the predecessor organization, the Dodge-Meigs Company, based at Axton (Axetown), had lumbered on both sides of the Raquette River upstream as far as Raquette Falls. There they built their main camp, which housed as many as 300 men at the peak of activity. From this base they harvested the huge virgin white pines and spruce along the upper reaches of the river of the forest to Cold River, one of the main tributaries. Thus over a period of less than ten years, the lumbermen had removed the choicest softwood from the northern and western slopes of the Seward Range.

The Santa Clara firm then started operations on the eastern side of the Range. This time the company made Ampersand Pond their headquarters and set up camps on both sides of that little lake which prior to the Civil War (1859) had been selected by William J. Stillman as the site for the celebrated Philosopher's Camp. This outing was of course later perpetuated by Emerson in his enthusiastic poetic tribute appropriately entitled "The Adirondacks."

Much of this land lay in what Verplanck Colvin in his report for 1897 called the Morse or Great Gore which was for generations the hotly disputed territory between what was termed the two northern boundaries of the Totten-Crossfield Purchase—more accurately—Jessup's Purchase from Totten and Crossfield.

Supposedly surveyed by Archibald Campbell in 1772, this tract crossed Upper Preston Pond, the Cold River headwaters, and then angled westerly to the south line of the Old Military Tract. This was roughly the boundary area between Franklin and Essex Counties.

In order to settle arguments constantly raging over various claims to ownership of this sizeable and valuable tract of forest land, Colvin personally ran a survey from Westport to the Bouquet River in New Russia. From there he established by sightline a point on the summit of the MacIntyre range. This he extended to the old line trees on Henderson and then down this line to Upper Preston Pond. In attempting to clear up the clouded titles, he also had to determine the south line of Township Twenty-Seven of MacComb's Purchase (Great Lot

1) which was supposed to be somewhere in the same general area. This of course only added further confusion to an already complicated situation. Moreover, three counties—Franklin, Hamilton and Essex—as well as the sovereign state of New York itself were all engaged in lively contention with each other and against the many private interests involved.

Although Colvin tried hard he never did get around to establishing mutually satisfactory boundaries. Therefore this area, which included Rondeau's Cold River country, was preempted by the Santa Clara Company. Starting with the Ampersand-Blueberry Pond section, this firm eventually, under the efficient control of Ferris J. Meigs, had a series of about eight camps extending down the valley to Long Lake.

Each of these camps had a crew of 70-90 men, who were paid from $30.00 to $35.00 per month and keep. To earn it they had a work-day which, during winter hauling season, started with a 2:30 a.m. breakfast and the logs were usually moving long before daylight. It was a no-nonsense, strictly—business outfit which insisted upon maximum output from the men and got it. No entertainment of any sort because by nightfall everyone was ready for the short night's sleep. No gambling and no goldbricking were tolerated. Nor was there ever time for hunting or fishing. Nor, unusual for a lumbering operation, was there ever any venison put on a table to cut down on the cost of meat.

Since some of the logging took place on the steep upper reaches of Ouluska Pass, getting the timber down required ingenuity and an innovation in procedure. This took the form of a huge drum around which was wound a three-quarter inch cable. The free end was attached by a hook to the loaded sleds and then paid out slowly to ease the loads down the incline. This single drum, although it had worked well in Western mines, proved ineffective, was shortly afterward abandoned and can still be seen high up in the Pass.

Soon afterward a system of four and even five drums, or Barringer Brakes as they were called, were used to lower the logs down to where the horsepower could safely be employed to haul the loads to the river banks or onto the ice, where they awaited the spring drive. A signal system, using bells, was rigged up to instruct the brakeman to either tighten up or ease off on the cable but despite all precautions loads occasionally got away. Cables sometimes snapped and the sleds rocketed downhill with the teamster wasting no time in jumping to safety. The legs of the horses would then get the full flaying effect of the flying cable before the hapless animals were crushed under an avalanche of logs.

Although Noah never worked for the Santa Clara Company he nevertheless trapped in the area and watched its operations from 1902 until 1922, when the project was finished.

First Outsiders Reach the Hermitage

Other than the loggers who were working in the region, there were very few people who ever visited the upper Cold River country. Those who did were usually hunters and fishermen who came in from Plumley's, some eleven miles away at the head of Long Lake Among the very first to visit the Hermitage were Dr. C. V. Latimer of Deposit, N. Y. and Jay L. Gregory, an insurance company executive from Binghamton. The two men met at Shattuck's Clearing in 1918; their affection for the Adirondacks generated a friendship which continued for over 30 years.

Around 1920, with the help of a woodsman, they built a well-hidden cabin on Cold River near where the Seward trail starts and about half-way between the Natural Dam (Miller's Falls) and the Big Eddy. Each year they, and occasionally their sons, spent two weeks fishing and the same length of time hunting deer in the Fall.

They first met Noah in 1926 but, since they were already thoroughly familiar with the section, never hired him as a guide. Very shy and rather distrustful of strangers, Noah kept the other party under surveillance for several years before he was convinced that they loved the woods every bit as much as he did. But once assured he soon dropped his reserved, sizing-up manner and they became longtime friends.

For many years Dr. Latimer, Jay Gregory, their sons and Noey hunted and fished together. For a number of years the two downstaters brought in presents of ammunition, boots, underwear and such food as he could use during the winter. In 1934 Noah reciprocated by rebuilding Camp Seward; the replacement held up well until the Big Blow of 1950 flattened it.

The Hermit, who in later years visited both men at their homes, was considered to be a thoroughly welcome and entertaining guest. The hosts have never forgotten the entrancing manner with which he regaled them with stories about Cold River animals, trails, streams and mountains. These recollections were of course much more meaningful because most of them were shared memories covering a long span of memorable years and long-past experiences.

Dr. Latimer still recalls Noah's delight upon seeing a framed enlargement of the photo which won Jay Gregory first prize in a contest sponsored by the New York *Herald* in 1929. Gregory labeled Noah the most courteous man he had ever met:—"Why, he's almost Chesterfieldian."

In addition to the ever-increasing number of sportsmen (including Irvin S. Cobb) whom Noah either guided or met, still another type of outdoorsman appeared on the Hermitage scene. These were hikers and mountain climbers who came in via the Northville-Placid trail.

The first known female visitors were Miss Little, a cousin of Dr. C. V. Lattimer, and her friend from Forest Hills, N. Y., in 1930. Betty Chatfield of Rochester arrived there in 1934, according to a dated photo in one of Noah's albums. Then came Mrs. Jay L. Gregory in October, 1936. In the summer of 1937 Grace Hudowalski and Louise Roark, the first two women 46ers, were guests at the Hermitage.

Ed Hudowalski and Rev. Ernest Ryder were apparently the first two climbers to meet Noah. They were climbing Couchie (Couchsachraga) when they were startled by the sound of axe blows. Investigating, they found it was Noah building himself an outpost on the mountainside. Noey, who knew his region like the proverbial book, gave the climbers some advice on the best approaches to the Seward Range—especially to Couchie—and often guided climbers to the peaks. In a letter he stated that he had climbed at least a hundred of the smaller peaks and declared that the views from many of them far exceeded those from the higher 4,000 footers.

In the Fall of 1937 the Troy 46ers made Noah an honorary member and thereafter Noah proudly wore the patch (designed by Ed Hudowalski) at the many shows where he was featured.

On July 3, 1938 a group from the Albany Chapter of ADK, consisting of the Hudowalskis, Nell Plum, Jack Benjamin, Orvil Gowie and others, officially welcomed him into that organization. Benjamin, who was killed in World War II, described the occasion in this manner: "Time for supper. Typical camp cookery augmented by speckled trout. Food eaten we approached the hour for our surprise. From one of the wigwams an ADKer (Grace H.) paraded in with a birthday cake made by Mrs. Catherine (Mother) Gowie aglow with candles Again that characteristic twinkle came into Noah's eyes as up from the table he jumped, grabbed the bearer by the arms and danced around holding the lighted cake before them. When the din had quieted somewhat he proceeded to open some of his numerous presents. He said little but his silence meant much.[1]"

After the presentation of the card the Hermit, speaking of his two mountain club associations said, "I could climb the highest mountain or go down in the lowest valley but nothing could please me more than these mountain lovers who have made me one of them. I never intended to join any fraternal organization but these people have taken me in and now they will have to put up with me[2]."

Nearly every year thereafter Grace[3] carried in an elaborately decorated cake, the gift of Mrs. Gowie. Even though his actual birthday was July 8th the timing never mattered—he celebrated whenever they arrived. On one occasion Noah reciprocated by sending Grace a cake on her birthday.

A. T. Shorey, another prominent member of the Adirondack Mountain Club, described a visit with Noah after an interval of three years. "It was pitch dark when we passed through the tepee gateway near Rondo's (sic) castle. A light was blinking through the trees. We skirted a small vegetable patch and came to two small shacks about head high. Hanging from a line stretched between the shacks were two white cloths labeled with charcoal "Welcome Adirondackers," "Welcome 46ers."

"Rondo heard us coming and his long bearded face was protruding from between the signs as we came up. He greeted the writer warmly and after my companions had been introduced, he escorted us along a narrow passage lined with big and little tepees. A bear's skull was perched on a small stump. At the entrance to the cooking tepee bears' paws were tacked.

[1] Jack T. Benjamin in the *Cloud-Splitter,* October, 1940, issue.
[2] Grace L. Hudowalski in *High Spots Yearbook,* 1939.
[3] Every time Grace, Ed and their friends visited Noah she always carried a cake in her hands — and by request a New York *Times* — the 18 miles in to the Hermitage.

"We settled down on seats before a fire in a very unique stone and sapling fireplace. A dishpan suspended over the fire caught and reflected most of the heat. It would seem that both the fireplace and the wigwam were in danger of catching on fire to produce the maximum of cheerfulness and glamor with safety.

"We talked of woods people and animals and fish for nearly an hour. The writer's friends who were experiencing Rondo's hospitality for the first time were thrilled and interested. They wondered at his ability to maintain himself so far from a "Five and Ten."

"It was the writer's first visit to Rondo after dark. To get the full startling effect of his camp it should be visited at night. There is something eerie in tall tepee poles with their tops lost in the lower branches of spruces and in the weird props all about such as bear skulls, axes and chopping blocks; and in the soft cultured voice of a little man with a black beard talking of simple woods experience and mixing with his talk a deal of philosophy and common sense. Rondo never brags. He is a forest gentleman in every way. If as Plutarch said, "Philosophy is the art of living," then Rondo is certainly a philosopher, for he has living down to its simplest elements. He needs little and asks for nothing. He is a friend to all who are friendly."[1]

Madeline Dodge, who was with the Dittmars on a trip to the Hermitage, still has vivid memories of one of Noah's evening violin concerts. Just before he started to tune up[2], he told the party not to make any sudden moves if visitors should be attracted by his music. Not long after he started to play they heard loud snorts in the shadows. Right afterward two large bucks emerged from the darkness and walked around among them. They then went back into the darkness. Soon afterward they returned accompanied by three does. Next to appear

[1] A. T. Shorey in I.O.C.S. Bulletin, August, 1940. Vol. 4 No. 4.
[2] His favorite tune, "The Irish Washer Woman."

were two spotted fawns. All seven graceful creatures moved freely about as Noah kept right on playing his fiddle in the firelight. A sudden movement by one of the human members of the audience sent the deer into instant flight back into the night.

About the same time still other members of the two mountain clubs also became frequent callers at Cold River City. Among these were Dr. Orra Phelps, Hal Burton, Hugh Flick, Karl Watson, Rudolph Wiezel, the Burguieres and Ed Harmes and his sons and the Dittmars, then of Ausable Forks. From that time on until just before and after his airlift to celebrity in February 1947, the number of visitors to Noah's Hermitage steadily mounted until there were more than 200 in a single season.

Following the Big Blow of November 25, 1950, the woods were closed to the public by a Conservation Department decree. Noah was therefore forced to absent himself from his Cold River haunts. But by then he had already passed his 67th birthday and knew full well that life and living at his beloved Hermitage had now become just a part of his past. He never went back again except in memory.

Rondeau versus Higher Authority

Although Noah John Rondeau was generally considered to be, as A. T. Shorey aptly characterized him, "a friend to all who were friendly," he could nevertheless become every bit as unfriendly—or even downright belligerent—toward those whom he had reason to distrust or dislike. Moreover, he was never the backslapping, hail-fellow-well-met type. Many people who later became recipients of his friendship have commented on his habit of constantly sizing them up, of pegging them or peering appraisingly over the top of his glasses and newspaper or book. In short they felt that they were under surveillance until they earned his partial confidence.

This can be at least partly explained by the fact that he never got over his feeling that he had been deprived of the opportunity to get a good education. Furthermore, he felt that he—as did many other members of minority groups, whether they were of Irish, Italian, Spanish or French-Canadian descent—were the innocent victims of much intentional as well as unintentional discrimination.

While those who were fortunate enough to get a better education and the accompanying improvement in living standards gradually sublimated this conditioned resentment, Noah never did. He always felt that he had been victimized—cheated out of something that should have been his birthright: a good schooling and a good income.

Whether it took the form of contempt for what he termed Big Fool American Big Business, inherited wealth, the election, welfare, economic and political systems in general—all these aspects of American life were more than somewhat suspect because they bewildered and infuriated him.

His journals are full of caustic comments and sometimes extended tirades on all these topics, but he saved his special scorn for everything having to do with Democrats. F. D. R. he labeled the traitor who sold out to Stalin and who was also responsible for the Great Depression. Harry S. Truman he verbally pilloried for firing MacArthur; and J.F.K., whom he labeled the spoiled brat of a millionaire's son, was weak because he failed to kick out Castro after mastering Khruschev in the Cuban missile crisis. His heroes were Eisenhower and Churchill. In fact his rancor often exceeded even that found in the usual source of many of his ideas—the *Daily News*.

Pungent though his comments may be in the cited instances, they were tame indeed compared with the torrent of terms he often unleashed against his twenty-year nemesis, the Conservation Department in general and several game protectors in particular. In this case, however, he was hardly the myopic Don Quixote tilting the windmills: he knew exactly who and what his enemies were and acted and reacted accordingly and understandably.

The lengthy feud with the Conservation Department apparently started about 1910, when Noah was living and barbering in Lake Placid. A brush fire presumably had gone out of control and burned over a vacant lot near his cabin. For some reason the Department accused Noah of being responsible for the minor conflagration and tried to collect from him the $9.00 which it cost them to put out the fire. Noah declared that he was innocent and would therefore not pay even .09. Although they kept dunning him for over two years, there is no evidence that he ever did pay up. But it was his first brush with the representatives of High Authority and from that time on he had no use for the Department.

The next confrontation occurred in 1920 and involved Noey and a game protector from Tupper Lake. At that time Noah was trapping muskrats along the Raquette River and so was the Warden. As the Hermit explained it to Linda Hart, who interviewed him in March, 1967:

"One day I started missing rats and knew that someone was stealing them. So I hid my boat and saw a C. C. employee take a muskrat from one of my traps[1]. I let him get away with it but I chased him down to the river to the stonecrusher landing. When I got there he was just getting into his car. He was then about 30 rods from the river. I hollered but he didn't hear me so I shot in the air, ran up to the car, threw down my gun, took off my coat and threw it down, picked up my gun and put it on him.

[1] Noah gave Peggy Byrne a different version of this incident. He told her that he had put one of his own rats into the protector's trap. Beforehand, however, he had marked it by notching one ear and scraping the calluses off its left foot.

He got out of his car and was so pale that he couldn't talk. I got in the car with him and we drove toward Tupper Lake. When we got to some houses he said 'Rondeau, you'll have to have an officer search this car!' So I got out and told him where my marks were on the muskrat...

"I 'published' quite a lot. I told the mailman and the Woodses at Axton about it. I also asked a man to phone someone. He did and everybody on the party line heard it. After a while the people kept kidding the Conservation man about it and he said that he'd show Rondeau what it was to try to ruin his reputation.

"So I wrote 30 pages telling him what I thought about his damaged reputation. "As for your good name," I wrote, "what you say is worth its weight in gold. And if all that gold was invested in cheesecloth it wouldn't be enough to make a garter for a hummingbird!" Then I wrote seven more pages on the subject of the Conservation Commission . . .

"Four years passed. Some of the crook's cousins were catching beaver out of season. They squeezed me out so I squawked on them. They swore to lies and tried to settle for two beaver instead of the nine they owed me. When they were in court I was the likely chief witness so the Conservation Commission man (the game protector) went to his chief with my four-year-old letter. They framed me to get me out of the way until the cousins got out of court. I was even charged with attempted murder in the first degree!

"Three weeks later I went out to Corey's, called them up and told them where I was. Pretty soon the Commission man and a policeman from Tupper Lake came and arrested me. This was May 11, 1924. The Commission man said that perhaps Mr. Rondeau was insane because he had lived alone in the woods so long. Accordingly I was examined by a jail doctor. There was a hearing at which I denied the charges. The Grand Jury did not sustain the charges so I was acquitted after 24 days with lice and bedbugs and no redress. Despite repeated applications I was unable to get a guide license from the Conservation Commission for more than 17 years.

"After the Malone experience I decided that I would never go into an American church to worship openly or cast an American vote until fully redressed—which I never have been and under the circumstances never expect to be."

In a February, 1967 interview Noah elaborated considerably on his incarceration experience in the Malone pokey and a subsequent trial. He declared that 75 of his friends doubled the $3,000.00 bail and that a dozen of them agreed to be his witnesses. On the day his case came up Malone seethed with bearded woodsmen. The courthouse was packed. After the judge had heard the charges and the Game Protector's testimony, His Honor asked Noah and his lawyer to come forward. Noah then announced that he would be his own lawyer, that he had 12 witnesses and that he would ask each one only two questions. The Judge then agreed to the procedure.

The first defense witness was a lumberjack from Saranac Lake who had known Noah for years. Noey faced him, hands in the pockets of his baggy pants and his brown eyes were fierce and intense.

"First question: Did I shoot at this man?"

"No," came the emphatic answer.

"Second question: How do you know?"

"Because," replied the lumberjack quietly, "If you had you would have killed him."

Eleven more witnesses took the stand and each gave exactly the same answers.

"Case dismissed!" roared the Judge.

The only thing wrong with this stirring story is that much of it just plain never happened—especially the tension-packed trial. It is a matter of record that Noah was actually arrested and that he did spend 22 days in the

Malone jail awaiting Grand Jury action because he could not raise the bail.

Proof of this is available in two articles which appeared in the Malone *Evening Telegram.* The first of these, dated May 13, 1924, gives the following information headlined: "Rondeau Held for Grand Jury. Trapper-preacher Accused of Firing on Game Protector. Noah J. Rondeau of Saranac Lake was placed under arrest at Corey's yesterday by Game Protector Wilkins[1] on a complaint that he had fired at him. Rondeau was brought to Malone and arraigned this morning before Justice of the Peace Moses H. Burno, at which time a charge of assault in the second degree was preferred. The defendant waived examination and was ordered held for action of the Franklin County Grand Jury. Rondeau was committed to the County Jail pending disposition by County Judge Paddock concerning amount of bail. Attorney John W. Genaway appeared for the defendant while District Attorney Harold W. Main represented the people."

"Rondeau, who is styled a trapper-preacher is alleged to have fired on the plaintiff in the woods in the vicinity of Tupper Lake recently. Rondeau got away in spite of the fact that officers had been searching for him since the offense, but they were unsuccessful until yesterday when it was learned that the accused had been seen near Corey's buying supplies. Upon tracking him a short distance into the woods, the Game Protector overtook him and placed him under arrest, bringing him to Malone today."

The second article dated June 4, 1924 reads as follows: "In the case of Noah J. Rondeau, whose case was considered by the Grand Jury, no indictment was found by that body so he was upon application made by his attorney—Francis B. Cantwell—discharged by the court. He at once returned to his home in Corey's. Rondeau was

---

[1] Fictitious name used at Rondeau's request.

before the Grand Jury on a charge of assault in the third degree."

The discrepancies in Noah's later recollections are obvious but nevertheless understandable. The first of these mishandlings of the facts is that his friends must not have managed to post the required bail money because if they had, Noah would of course never have spent any time in jail.

The second misrepresentation relates to his appearance before the Trial Jury later in the year. This of course was impossible because, since the Grand Jury had already cleared him, there was no reason for such a trial. A short time later he reportedly indulged his strong sense of vindictiveness by sending Wilkins a fistful of bullets to remind him of trap thieves.

Rondeau's Third Encounter with the Law

Nearly two years after the Hermit's unpleasant experience in Malone, he found himself again in court—this time in Saranac Lake. The story was well covered in a news item which was carried in the November 23, 1926 issue of the *Adirondack Enterprise* and rated front page treatment, left-hand column. The main headline stated: "Hermit Held Not Guilty of Game Law Violations." The sub headline declared: "Defendant Tries His Own Case in Most Unusual Trial Seen Here." The story coverage itself was as follows:

"What will probably be the last chapter in the Noah J. Rondeau affair was enacted this morning in Justice Court when the diminutive hermit emerging from his solitary retreat at Corey's was found not guilty of a game law violation by a jury.

"Rondeau was charged with having possessed the hide of a wild deer without evidence of sex attached and he had insisted upon his right to a trial by jury on this comparatively minor offense.

"Rondeau elected to forego the services of a lawyer and

tried his own case before Justice of the Peace Seaver A. Miller. Although he showed little knowledge of the law and court practice, he did reveal a surprising degree of resourcefulness and readiness of wit.

"Game Inspector Ray L. Burmaster prosecuted the case for the State and the only witnesses were Game Protector Carl A. Wilkins, who was the complainant and Albert Hathaway of Corey's, who Rondeau declared had sold him the deerskin.

"The trial was featured by an effort on Rondeau's part to get before the jury his contention that the complaint against him was part of an affair between himself and growing out of the theft of a Muskrat from one of Rondeau's traps, which theft Rondeau blamed on Wilkins. Rondeau was interrupted several times in this attempt, and at one time told the court that he had thought this trial was his opportunity to bring out the whole story. In summing up for himself, he delved into past history to a considerable extent.

The seizure of the deer hide, it was brought out, took place on May 11, 1924 when Protector Wilkins visited Rondeau's cabin at Corey's and placed Rondeau under arrest on a warrant charging assault second degree. Wilkins was the complainant on his warrant and accused Rondeau of firing at him with a gun. Rondeau was subsequently discharged by the grand jury at Malone when no indictment was found against him.

"In the meantime action had been postponed on the seizure of the deer skin, and the warrant for Rondeau's arrest on the game law violation was served only recently.

"The deer skin which the game protectors claimed had been seized at Rondeau's cabin was entered as evidence and was carefully examined by the jury.

"The jury in the case was composed of M.L. Carey, G. A. Bombard, H. A. Thompson, William Pasho, Charles Cochrane and John Liscomb. The not guilty verdict was returned after a deliberation of about 15 minutes."

Over the ensuing years Noah had plenty of time to renew and review his traumatic confrontations with Higher Authority. In all likelihood he decided to revamp the facts in the Malone clash in order to produce a more favorable image. It was not so much a case of tampering with the truth as it was ingenuity and alteration. Knowing that his listeners expected a good story, he made it an even better one. As Pooh-Bah in Gilbert and Sullivan's *Mikado* phrased it so cleverly: "It is merely corroborative detail intended to give artistic verisiltude to an otherwise bald and unconvincing narrative."

By this time it is easy to figure out why Rondeau felt that he was being persecuted by the Game Law Enforcers. That feeling festered even more when still another Protector tried to frame him. This time N. J. R. had gone deerhunting with Sam Shaw and Charlie Tyler of Corey's. During the day Noah shot an eight-point buck, which he hung up in the woods. Then he and the others went into Shaw's place to celebrate and play cards. Not long afterward, there was a knock on the door. Sam opened it and saw a Game Warden, who asked for Rondeau. Noah stepped out and was told that he was under arrest for shooting a doe. The outraged man denied having done so and declared that he had indeed shot a deer but that it was an eight-point buck.

The Warden and the three other men then went to the place where the deer had been hung up. There they found that someone—probably the Warden himself since he and Noah were anything but friends—had substituted an illegal doe. But when Shaw and Tyler protesting, verified Noah's statement that they had been with him when he had shot the buck and agreed to act as his witnesses in court if necessary, the Warden wisely decided to drop the charge.

Noah had still another reason for his chip-on-the-shoulder attitude toward Higher Authority as represented by the Conservation Department. In order to assure himself of shelter in remoter areas during the hunting and trapping seasons, the Hermit had built several strategically well concealed shacks. These were eventually found by the Department men and summarily burned down. This of course skyrocketed Noah's blood pressure and gave two more reasons for hating the Department.

"They kep' on houndin' me and framin' me up," he complained to a friend, "just because I made the mistake of being too religious. Why for 35 years I was so conscientious that I refused to eat short trout even when someone caught and cooked them for me. They spied on me a lot, and I knew it but they never caught me with illegal game, never—not a once.[1] They seen for themselves the one bear and one deer I shot every Fall and hung up to cure, freeze and chop off what I needed all Winter. They came snoopin' and seen my little garden—turnips and potatoes and flowers mostly."

Once Noah invited them in to taste slam-bang, the everlasting stew, a nameless concoction that simmered on the back of the stove all year and was periodically perked up by adding an onion, potato, partridge or rabbit whenever the level went down. But the stew was far too nondescript and gamey for them to identify.

Nor did Noah's face behind the great growth of bushy whiskers ever give them a clue. But the Frenchiness in him, the delight in games and jokes made his brown eyes dance in glee. "Guess, go on now, guess what's in the pot! But I ain't agoin' to say."

As far as the Conservation Department was concerned, its law enforcement division considered that, while Noah was living in the Gore and therefore on disputed land, he was nevertheless more than somewhat of a nuisance. Although they entertained strong suspicions that he was an out and out outlaw, and even though they kept

---

[1] Noah's own words to an interviewer shed further light on his extra-legal activities: "I played the game safe and I've had a lot of that stuff (out of season fish and game) and never got caught. They've got to do that yet — and they ain't got much hope or time left either!"

him under constant surveillance, the Game Protectors assigned were never able to get enough valid evidence to establish an airtight case. All through the years he was a sharp thorn in their sides and there was a continuous matching of wits.

By burning the two shacks at either end of his trap-line they apparently felt that they had found an effective way to force him out, but resourceful Noah vehemently termed the destruction of his property as just another skirmish and refused to pull out. In this case he found strategically located hollow logs or dug holes in sand-banks or steep slopes, stuffed them with leaves and marsh hay and used them as snug, temporary shelters. These along with well-stashed emergency food caches enabled him to survive when away from the Hermitage.

The Department also claimed that Rondeau was guiding without a license. About 1925, when the feud with the Game Protectors was at its height, the Conservation Department refused to issue him a permit. A decade later, the Hermit of course did guide many aspiring 46ers but apparently did not consider leading parties to the Seward Range and Couchie summits to come under the heading of guiding. Since he did receive presents if not actual pay, the Conservation Department officials maintained that this constituted breaking the law.

Another source of concern for the Department was Noah's known carelessness with fires, a particularly nasty habit shared by many other old-timers. Even though he may have felt that he was fully aware of the dangers involved and had taken the necessary precautions to contain his wigwam fires, he nevertheless left them untended much of the time. Nor is this accusation based solely on the allegations of the Rangers and the Wardens: several of his friends have also made the same critical comment.

The Department also was not happy about his cutting down numerous trees in order to feed his fires.

Whenever he could Noah never overlooked a chance to make life as lively as possible for those in the Conservation Department for whom he harbored a particularly profound resentment. But for all of them he made it quite clear that their presence on Hermitage property represented what he considered to be trespassing. He advertised this by displaying a large Turkish towel on which he had painted this admonition—NO GAME PROTECTORS ALLOWED! And on the door of the Town Hall he also nailed a similar warning but in smaller print.

This long-lasting feud with the Conservation Department also included anyone in law-enforcement uniform. Even as late as 1954 when the Hermit had an exhibit at the Wilmington Sportsmen's Show, he and Higher Authority were still leery of each other. One day two State Troopers put in their appearance and wondered aloud about the contents of a kettle simmering over a small stove. He pretended that they weren't there so finally one of the unwanted visitors spoke up. "Say, Rondeau, what's in the kettle? And just how many deer do you kill each year?" . . . . .

A month after Seagear's confab with Rondeau[1] a group from the Albany *Knickerbooker News* "discovered" N. J. R. Right after Labor Day city editor Charles L. Mooney; Julius Heller, court reporter; Frank T. McCue, promotion manager and Charles A. Smakwitz, Eastern representative of Warner Bros., made the long trip in to the Hermitage. When they finally arrived at Noah's diggings, they got their first in a series of surprises. "An old fellow came out, said 'Hello, gentlemen,' and informed us that we would have to sign the guest register. We wondered if we had heard correctly and asked "Did you say guest register?" Assured that we had heard him correctly I remarked that I thought he was

---

[1] See introduction for particulars on this interview.

supposed to be a Hermit. He replied 'I am but what's the use in being a Hermit if you don't meet a lot of people?'

Mooney, in his Sept. 11th article on the interviews, went on to say: "We have always prided ourselves on our ability to spot a phony but we must admit that from time to time down through the years N. J. R. has had us baffled. Webster defines a Hermit as a person who retires from society and lives in solitude. It couldn't be said that Rondeau did exactly that because, when we looked over his larder, discovered it to be well stocked and expressed surprise over it, Rondeau explained: 'Oh people are always dropping me off all kinds of food!'

"When he took his bow and arrow in hand, however, we had a somewhat different feeling. He told us that he hadn't shot it in years and the rusty arrows certainly didn't belie it. We asked him to shoot it for a picture so he hung up an old washcloth on a bush, stepped back 50 yards and pulled back on the 8 foot bow. The arrow bored cleanly through the cloth and, just to prove that it wasn't a lucky shot, the Hermit proceeded to send a second arrow neatly through the small target . . .[1]

"Rondeau, a different kind of Hermit from the popular conception, is voluble on every subject except the one most important to the interviewer. 'How did you happen to become a Hermit?' I asked.

"And how did you happen to become a newspaper man?' Rondeau politely replied and would say no more.

"Noah never grows lonely and that incidentally is a question he has been called upon to answer hundreds of times.

'All my friends ask that,' he said. 'I tell them that

[1] The arrows were capped with empty cartridge shells and tipped with razor-edged bits of steel taken from an old bucksaw blade.

During a radio broadcast over WNBZ (Saranac Lake) made prior to the trip to N.Y.C., Noah discounted the report that he took all his game a' la Robin Hood. He said that he had not used these weapons for 6 years since he considered his rifle to be far more effective. His journals show that he had killed a bear, two deer, many raccoons and rabbits and an occasional pesky chipmunk with the primitive weapon.

loneliness is only a state of mind. Some people can be lonelier in a crowded railroad station than I am right here in my woods.'

"One of the legends was recalled about Noah that a disappointment in love had influenced his decision to become a hermit. 'Never had a woman in my life,' he told us. 'Never did like women around. They talk only once a day—from morning 'til night. And besides they want to boss a man around. They sometimes want to bring their mother to live with you. No, sir, no women for this chicken! !'

"Noah, it developed, is interested in goings-on in the outside world and for a hermit, is remarkably well posted. He displays a lively interest in and a somewhat technical knowledge of the atomic bomb. 'I feel that the atomic bomb hastened the end of the war,' he said. He accents the first syllable of atomic. 'I've read up a good deal on atomic power and in a way I was sorry they made an instrument of war out of it. But the way it saved so many of our boys' lives I guess it was a good thing.'

"By no means an isolationist, as he explains it, Noah nevertheless believes that this country is too concerned about other countries. 'Take Russia,' he said, 'I've been reading where some folks have been deploring the fact that we can't seem to understand the Russians. What do we want to understand them for? I'm not interested in Russia. They don't even speak the same language. Let the Russians stay in Russia. I'll stick right here . . .

" 'As for education some of these kids nowadays who want to quit school make me sick. I've been on my own since I was a little shaver. Practically everything I know I picked up myself. I never could make enough money to get to college but I'd like to have made it.'

"Noah takes a lively interest in politics but he hasn't voted in 35 years. 'Too much fuss getting set to go to the polls,' he explained. 'Only takes a second to vote and then I have to hoof it back 25 or 30 miles!'

"Here is a strange character: a man who shut himself away voluntarily; a man who has had little schooling yet has a good command of English; a man who likes folks who come to visit him and who loves the woods in which he lives. 'I want to die right here in my wood,'[1] he told us. 'I can't see going outside to live now. I'm too old to make a living. I only hope I can stay here—I like it!' "

The Seagears article, followed by those which appeared in the *Knickerbocker News,* generated a great deal of interest in the Mayor of Cold River City and undoubtedly influenced the rapid succession of events which culminated in his air-lift to nation-wide fame and his subsequent departure from his beloved valley.

---

[1] It is noteworthy that Noah spent several weeks during that summer clearing and leveling his gravesite. He spent long hours selecting rounded white stones and several suitable slabs from the bed and banks of Cold River to improve the appearance of the plot. His final resting place, however, was the North Elba Cemetery, near Lake Placid.

THE AIR LIFT TO FAME

During the waning months of 1946 the top brass of the Conservation Department, acting on the advice of Clayt Seagears, decided to feature Rondeau at the upcoming National Sportsmen's Show to be staged at Grand Central Palace in New York City. William E. Petty, chief ranger and forester for the northern region, was instructed to contact N.J.R. and make the necessary arrangements. Therefore on Jan. 10, 1947 the following message was air-dropped to the Hermit:

Dear Mr. Rondeau:

The Conservation Department would like to have you go down to the Sportsmen's Show in New York City February 15th to 23rd. They will pay your expenses and also pay you $100.00 for the week. They would like you to bring along your bow and arrows and buckskin suit. Do not know where this will land but if you will go will you wave down near the Dam or spell out YES in big enough letters on the snow so I can read it. Come out a few days earlier than the 15th and plan on staying with me at Headquarters, Saranac Inn. Call me when you get out and I will pick you up wherever you come out.

William E. Petty

What happened next is best related in a New York City newspaper, dated Jan. 15, 1947, which carried the following story: "Bearded Noah Rondeau, Cold River hermit who for three decades has lived by bow and arrow in his Adirondack Mountain hideout, plans to visit New York. Wears deerskin garment with bearclaws and teeth for buttons. He was contacted by plane by William Petty, chief ranger and forester, after it was decided by members of the Conservation Department that they would like the recluse to appear at the Sportsmen's Show.

"Petty, who figured that it would have taken four days to make the thirty-six miles round trip on snow-shoes, contacted Melvin Boettcher at Saranac Airport. A small plane warmed up and in 55 minutes Petty and the pilot were back with a yes answer from Rondeau. An invitation attached to a tiny parachute was dropped near the Hermitage. It also had instructions to Rondeau to tramp out yes or no in the snow.

"Petty also dropped a pound of bacon and a pound of butter. The men in the plane spotted ten deer, three near Rondeau's place. Rondeau waved coat in greeting from the roof of his cabin."

According to his diary, because of the deep snow and the difficulty in getting out, Noah declined the first invitation. He went into a huddle with himself during which he made a profound reappraisal of the Department. "For years they had been wonderful to me," he remarked later on. "Besides, the ones I had been thinking of were the old crowd and they were all dead now."

But when the plane kept returning during the next few weeks Noah could not help wondering why Petty seemed so persistent. He could not quite figure out why they were making such a fuss over him. What he didn't find out until a month later was the Conservation Department had anticipated his acceptance and that they were already building a replica of his Town Hall in Grand Central Palace. Moreover, they had even advertised his appearance and had scheduled him for a national radio broadcast.

The next message assured Noah that he would not have to concern himself about getting out through the deep snows that fell after his acceptance of the invitation. On Feb. 11th, he was informed that they would come in after him the next day. In the midmorning of the 12th, according to Noah, the helicopter came down "as gently as a honeybee on a posy." But he also added that "They came darn near spoilin' my snow."

On the first two of the required nine round trips in from Saranac Lake four men, one of them John Wingate, came and went. "Pictures, Recordings and News Reels," noted Noah in his journal for that day. The Hermit and his props—bearskin, traps, snowshoes, bow and arrows etc. filled the small cabin of the chopper on one of the final trips out. His diary entry states: "3 p.m. I fly over Ampersand Mountain. Over 200 wait for me in 21 below zero weather at Saranac Air Field. I talk on phone to C. B. Seagears in New York."

At the Airport, which at that time consisted of just a field and rough shack which served as the terminal building, Bill Harvey of Saranac Lake took charge. As local manager he had already made arrangements with Colonial Airline president, Sigmund Janis, who was enthusiastically aware of the publicity value of the occasion. Therefore Noey was welcomed aboard as the guest of the company. Hans Groenhof, company photographer, took a full set of pictures of the arrival of the chopper and the DC3, Noah's being bussed by Renee Le Beau, attractive French Canadian hostess and the take off of the silver bird for the Big City,[1] at 4 p.m. on Feb. 14th.

At 5:45 Noah and his entourage arrived at LaGuardia Field. There, a crowd of reporters and photographers awaited him and he registered great delight at the enthusiastic reception before being driven first to the Grand Central Palace and then to the Belmont Plaza, his hotel for the week. . .

A morning edition of one of the metropolitan papers described his arrival in this fashion: "Toting the homemade bow and arrows he used to kill game for food,

[1] Rondeau was apparently fascinated by planes, used to spend long hours at the Saranac Airport pumping Bill Harvey, a pilot himself, about planes and flying. The Hermit especially liked to see the ships land and take off. One day as one of them slowly broke out its landing gear as it circled the field, Noah exclaimed, "Well, there she is afixin' to light."

This observation is in the same league as the late Harry Williams' (Upper Saranac Lake) remark when asked if he could repair a battered guideboat. "Well, I won't guarantee to fix it up but I can sure linger its life a little."

bearded Noah John Rondeau, 63-year-old Adirondack Mountain recluse, is in town to appear at the National Sportsmen's Show opening today.

"Rondeau, who was flown out of his snowbound camp by helicopter Wednesday, had his first glimpse of New York City since 1920 when he arrived by plane last night.[1] The hermit, who has lived alone for more than 20 years, brought along his snowshoes and deerskin suits. He was clad in a greatcoat and muskrat cap. Rondeau said he planned to visit Hayden Planetarium while visiting the city. 'I'm interested in astronomy; also biology and geology,' he explained.

The purpose behind Noah's appearance at the Show and the impression created by him are best described by Seagears himself, because he was the person who with Bill Petty originally thought up the idea of having him displayed. According to him, Rondeau was there to help sell the need to retain the wilderness character of New York State's Forest Preserve and to show it is possible in the most heavily populated state in the nation to live in primitive wilderness, how to protect it and enjoy it.

"N.J.R. immediately adapted himself to the city. He ate $3.00 steak dinners, stayed up until 2 a.m., was kissed by movie stars (Arlene Whelan among them), spoke on 14 radio broadcasts and on We The People, a television show; signed thousands of autographs, became exposed to trillions of germs, rode in big planes and small ones, made three newsreel shorts, wore store clothes and talked nearly 16 hours a day. Never once was he confused, outwardly irritated or ill.

"His one lesson to all of us—and a great one, is this: Use your natural resources wisely and they'll use you

[1] The reason for that trip was to try to market several inventions. He stayed with some wealthy friends at Douglaston, L. I., went into Manhattan a couple times but didn't like the looks of the place. Too much hustlin' and bustlin' and all helter-skelter to suit him. Figuring that the fellows he was going to see would hornswoggle him anyway, he gave up the idea, took in the usual tourist sights and went back home again.

well. Take out only what you need. Help put back what you take. See more in hunting than just the harvest, more in fishing than the fading spots on a dying trout, more in the future of your outdoors than the bare hills, gully scars and muddy waters. Shake hands with the guy. He's helping America learn something. He's a colorful and highly intelligent conversationalist."

Evidence that the story of Noah and his transition from hermit of Cold River to Exhibit A at Grand Central Palace took place almost immediately. Frank Bruce, formerly of Tupper Lake and a newspaper man in the South, wrote that clippings of the story and photos of him were even carried in a Tuscaloosa, Alabama paper. A.P. and Wirephoto coverage spread the story from coast to coast. There were probably a half dozen accounts at least which came through during that week, he wrote. "I heard of the progress being made in getting him out of the wilderness by helicopter both over the radio and in the press and then a story came through that the trip was successful. Every detail of this experiment was covered from the time the plane flew over his cabin and dropped the invitation right through his jaunt to New York. This was probably the biggest publicity story to come out of either Tupper Lake or Saranac Lake in the fourteen years I have been away.

"Frankly I was disappointed to see Saranac get the date-lines because we all know that Rondeau considered Tupper his second home. Perhaps the lack of an airport to allow the newspapermen to fly there made the difference."

The lack of an airport did make a difference but the fact is that the story "broke" out of Saranac Lake because the entire project was handled by the State Conservation Department through its district office there and as a result the news releases all originated in that place.

During the week's run of the Show Noah thoroughly enjoyed being the featured attraction. He met thousands of people, including many who had seen him at the Hermitage, and was unquestionably the talk of the town. Nor did he overlook the pecuniary possibilities of the situation. He got a quarter each for his autographs and a half dollar for signed postcard photos. Noticing that some people were tossing money between the boards of the upturned keg he was using for a stool, he providently provided a larger receptacle—his packbasket. This he stuffed with leaves and seeded with folding money as a suggestion, and the gratifying sight of the green hummock of bills often overflowed the brim of the basket.

Before leaving the city he was, in response to popular request, again on We The People. When the Show closed Noah had only a few days' rest in Saranac Lake before setting out for Albany. There he was again the main attraction. In covering the show Spec Fowler of the *Times Union* made the following observations and comments: "Rondeau is remarkably well (self) educated and speaks softly and clearly. In his quiet way and with no fanfare or gale from a 60 mile an hour Master of Ceremonies, he serenely goes his own way, the lion of the Albany show just as he was in the New York City affair. He is as gentle with the foolish questions asked by adults as he is with the bug-eyed yelps which pop from the small fry when they see his uncivilized appearance. Noah, in case you don't know, is a clean man even though he could hardly be considered amongst the ten best dressed."

As far as the Hermit was concerned the highlight of his Albany visit was the red carpet treatment given him on a conducted tour of the Conservation Department Headquarters and his hobnobbing with thirty-two state senators. Primed with three Manhattans he saw himself on the film taken at Cold River and later addressed the Rotary Club at the Ten Eyck Hotel.

After another short respite at Saranac Lake the Hermit hit the road again, this time to Rochester and Buffalo, where he also made radio broadcasts and speeches to various organizations. The next two seasons he starred at shows in Utica, Saratoga, Syracuse and Boston (February, 1949) for fees ranging from $550 to $800 per appearance.

He was also the cynosure of attention at Saranac Lake in 1949 and again in 1950 when he crowned the Carnival king and queen and rode a float in the parade. Other bookings included shows at Tahawus, Schenectady, Amsterdam, Oxford, Luzerne, Rouses Point and the Essex County Fair at Westport.

In 1951 he made a return appearance at the New York City Sportsmen's Show and soon afterward was featured for the third time on We The People. Later in the year he worked at Frontiertown and was Santa Claus at the North Pole. From that time on his drawing power waned somewhat until 1954, when he set up his Town Hall replica and accompanying props for the summer-long run of the Whiteface Mountain Sportsmen's Show at Wilmington.

Having tasted success and finding it both gratifying and enjoyable, Noah tried persistently to prolong his stay in the limelight. He wrote numerous letters to the booking agent of the World of Fun and was also unsuccessful in his efforts to sign up with the prestigious American and Canadian Sportsmen's Show organization. But, except for occasional unremunerative engagements at service groups and fish and game clubs, requests for Noah's services as a public entertainer were now almost nil. Although this was an understandably deep disappointment to him, his four brief but rewarding years of exposure to fame nevertheless furnished him with a free-flowing reservoir of evergreen memories to draw on during his declining days.

THE FINAL YEARS

Although Rondeau had thoroughly relished his relatively short exposure to fame, he nevertheless longed to get back to his Cold River solitude. Taking time out from his efforts to line up more bookings in late 1948, he returned to the Hermitage for the periods from June 27—August 9; then again from August 26 to November 3. Later that autumn he spent three weeks with Frank Blanchard, caretaker at Ampersand Park. During this time he revisited the Cold River valley, hunted and otherwise savored the wilderness life.

In late November of that year Noah with the help of several Rangers, packed up about 600 pounds of his belongings and toted them the nearly five miles of the Northville-Placid Trail to its junction with the truck road. On this trip Noah's burden was his cherished rocking chair. This, with the rest of his riches, were hauled out to the Conservation Department headquarters at Saranac Inn for temporary storage.

After a winter at 4 Alpine Terrace in Saranac Lake, punctuated by a trip to the Boston Sportsmen's Show in February, Noah again returned to Cold River City at the end of April for another sojourn. In his journal he set down the following reaction: "April 29th I walk about my Town Hall and City. Robins and Juncos, Chipmonks and Sparrows. No Gas Stations, no Dogs on every Corner, no Church Bells in my Ears, What freedom alone in natural primitiveness and what unsatisfactory waste in living Civilization, serving Gods, Religions and industrial Slavery and multiplicity of useless fool subjects. I find lost manuscript (Recollection of 60 years). 11 o'clock Air Plane drop 37 packages in my Briars. I gather supplies all day. Sundown—Deer at 1st Brook, above Dam—and 5 deer—tails gallop east in Dead Flow. Nighthawks screech. No mice at Cold River City and very few Barred Owls."

Except for two trips out he stayed at his diggings until November 23rd, when he left for his winter quarters in Saranac Lake . . .

The next May he set up his Town Hall replica and wigwam at the Corey's crossroads and made trips to shows at St. Regis Falls, Oxford, Marathon and Malone.

On August 11, 1950 he moved his exhibit to North Pole at Wilmington, where he also worked as the substitute Santa Claus. On November 7th Noah made his farewell trip to Cold River. This time he went by way of Tupper and Long Lake, where he left his supplies with the Helms brothers to be flown in later. When two deer hunters arrived and wanted transportation to Plumley's camp at the head of the lake, Noah joined forces with them in chartering the four-passenger seaplane.

Upon reaching his much-missed bailiwick he burned the old bough bed, washed all dishes, got two armfuls of blue joint hay and made himself a Cold River feather bed. It took him nearly two days to make the Town Hall function in city style, and in due time his "finger bowls and paper napkins" arrived by air and were dumped into the briars. He was now right at home and soon made the mice recognize his authority.

The mountains and the valley forest seemed especially beautiful that autumn; they meant so much to him because he knew every tree like a flying squirrel. On Nov. 14th he shot a big buck from the door of the Town Hall. The deer was across the river and quite some distance away, but Noey had seen the sun glint from his antlers as he pussyfooted among the trees. He shot three times although the first bullet, as he found on inspection, had made two of the shots unnecessary. He caught two bullets in the thorax and before the echo of the shots reached Seward Brook, the deer was dead on the snow. Twelve points and over 200 pounds.

During the evening of Nov. 24th the advance winds of the Big Blow made Noah uneasy, so the next day he started back by way of his shortcut through Ouluska Pass. When he reached the Amperand Park boundaries he found little evidence of the havoc, for there were no trees across the road. But west of the Park along the four-mile stretch to Stony Creek bridge the beautiful forest was a jackstraw jungle of slash six feet or more in depth. Three caretakers from Avery Rockefeller's, a dozen hunters and about 20 Conservation Department men took two days to cut out that section of the road. Most of the familiar landmarks had been obliterated so he could hardly tell where he was. In every direction he could see only yellow birches still standing, braced by the slash and with their broken limbs dangling.

A later assessment of the damage caused by the unprecedentedly destructive storm showed that more than 400,000 acres had been seriously affected—from 25 to 100 per cent leveled. So vast was the area and so great was the danger of subsequent fires that the whole region was closed to the public for more than three years. That edict, plus the realization that he was then at 67 too old to ever seriously consider the resumption of the uncertain ways of the wilderness, ended forever that phase of Rondeau's life.

Moreover, having found that living outside, even though monotonous, was nevertheless more predictable and less precarious, he made a slow adjustment to changing situations and living quarters. From Saranac Lake, where he spent nearly a year, he moved to Wilmington; then to Ausable Forks, where he resided for most of the second year (1952) with his sister, Priscilla McCasland. At various times he roomed and boarded in Haselton and Wilmington.

During that period he spent the winter of 1954-5 with L. H. Gillies and family in Birmingham, Alabama. The two had known each other and had guided and hunted together often in the Massawepie-Conifer area as far back as 1905.

Still later he lived with Abe Fuller on the River Road in Lake Placid and finally in the place he liked best of all—Singing Pines, a cabin surrounded by pines and birches on the road from Wilmington to Upper Jay.

Singing Pines, owned by Dick Smith of Lake Placid, who had hunted and trapped with Noah and had known him for nearly thirty years, was an ideal place for the Hermit to live out his last three years. The indulgent owner let Noey build another gate to the city, wigwams and a flower and vegetable garden.

Then too he built a tepee and worked several days a week for Madeline Dodge, of Wilmington, who had also been a Cold River visitor years before and had a great deal of affection and admiration for him.

There too Rondeau's friends of other years as well as newer ones could and did visit him often. They all agreed that it was just like old times. The rooms were just as smoky and every bit as cluttered as they had been at the Hermitage.

Even though Noah had become too worn-out to do much more than take short walks in the woods with a gun during hunting season, he nevertheless savored reminiscing about his hunting successes—especially with those men who had shared the experiences with him. One of those trips most frequently relived was a jaunt with Smith, who was with him and vouches for its accuracy. On this particular day the two friends were walking cautiously down an abandoned tote road. Suddenly they jumped a sizeable buck which crossed the opening in two long bounds and seemingly disappeared into a dense clump of evergreens. Reacting very rapidly Rondeau brought down his .35 caliber rifle from his shoulder and fired four fast shots. Almost immediately afterward they heard the deer flounder and then fall. Going over to the spot the hunters found that three of the shots were clustered just behind the front shoulder of a ten-pointer.

Another testimonial, this one not to his hunting but to his speaking ability, affords additional indication of his versatile nature.

From *The Record Post*, AuSable Forks, April 5, 1951:

The Jay-Wilmington Brotherhood

"When I heard that Noah Rondo, an Adirondack hermit, was to address the Brotherhood, well, says I, in my ignorance, and what for a speech can a man like that make? I thought for sure we were in for a wild and wooly palaver, an explosion of backwoods bologna. But says I, I can stand anything once. Well, says I, not many will come, and it will be just as well. But a big crowd came, much to my surprise. In due time, Dr. Dittmar was asked to introduce the speaker, which he did handsomely; as if he were introducing a royal prince. Why all this wind, thought I, just for a hermit? But when that bewhiskered, straightlaced, smily man stood up, made his bow, just as perlite like as a college professor, Johnnie Jones[1] was taken down two pegs, maybe three. He had never seen a more likely-looking man than that hermit; a pippin of a man with a face as smily as the full moon. This gave a new twist to my idea of hermits. Well sir, I'm telling you, when he got up steam, he talked like a whirlwind, and what he said was real smart and interesting. My ears burned and my heart thumped to hear that man describe his lonely one-man town at Cold River. And I tell you, hermit or no hermit, he had a powerful flow of oratory, and made us all feel at home in his forest retreat. He couldn't ask us to sit down 'cause he hasn't a chair on his ranch. Says I, one thing is sure, he'll never wear out the seat of his pants a sittin'. He tuk us right into his confidence, and told us just how he maneuvers, how he gets

---

[1] Penname of N. S. Pinney of Jay, N. Y.

his provisions, and how he keeps them from spiling without an ice box. It was all as strange and curious as a woman's bonnet, and them gestures were more eloquent than his words, they made us all snicker. I'll tell the world, he didn't live in them woods for nothing. No speaker ever knowed his subject, or waxed more gloriously over it than he. Why, when he was speaking, it seemed as if he was vocalizing the mystic spirit of the woods.

"Never have I seen a man so chuck full of nature. I suppose his pep was due to breathing so long that fresh, balsamic air. He has certainly developed a charm city folks might envy. His vein of humor was big as an elephant, and quite as tricky; nothing sleep-producing about that speech. His laugh was as contagious as the measles. Well, Sir, some laughed so hard they bust the buttons off their coats. But I could plainly see that beneath his frolicking humor there lurked a soul of rare sincerity and worth. No louse in the governor's hat was ever more happy in his environment than is that hermit in his. How stimulating and youthfulizing his daily work must be! His liniments were all aglow with joy and sweet content. I suppose his making love to dame nature made him that way. Such people never grow sour or old. I once heard the professor say that nature is our oldest and best teacher, and when I heard that man spill his knowledge like beans, I'm blamed if I don't agree. He knows nature like a woodchuck. I've formed a notion that no man, hermit or no hermit, has compassed life or comprehended himself without communing with that great teacher. The village fool could see that Noah Rondo has learned some rich lessons from her. Never did I suspect that living a secluded life in a pine forest could result in such deep larning. The thought slowly soaked into my consciousness that there is a real and solid wisdom to be found in the pathless woods, and that our speaker has graduated from this unique school with a magna cum laude degree. I guess them Latin words mean he got there with both feet!

"Noah Rondo says he don't need a radio to tell him about Carter's Little Liver Pills or Lydia Pinkham's Elixir of Life, as he don't need any sich. Why in thunder should he wade knee deep through such deep grass for a little entertainment, when he can bathe his soul any time with such heavenly music as the booming of the partridge, the pathos of the wood-dove's cry, the spirit rapping of the prospecting woodpecker, the purling brook as it rambles on chattering with its banks, the cry of the hungry nestling in the tree tops, the sweet bird songs, and the moaning of the wind among the pines? All other music is imitative.

"Nor does he lack for company when he is in daily contact with deer, bears, foxes, squirrels, rabbits, winged creatures galore, and other denizens of the forest, to all of which he is friend and brother, and with which he holds sympathetic communion. His table, also, is loaded with such viands as brook trout, venison, and other woodland goods that make one's mouth water.

Think, also, of the majestic scenery with which he is surrounded: lordly mountain peaks, peaceful valleys, grassy plains, long cathedral aisles of mossy loveliness, leading thru the forest, deep, tawny pools of sparkling water amid overarching foliage, where water spiders swim and blue dragon flies poise in the leafy shade, flanked with dim temples of cedar, and pine palaces. Who would not luxuriate and grow wise, and feel real content in such a haven?

"He described his winters as long and rather tedious, but when old King Winter knocks at his door, he is ready for him and bids him welcome. He says to him:—

"Bite, frost, bite;
You roll up away from the light the blue wood-louse,
And the plump dormouse.
The bees are stilled, the flies are killed,

And you bite far into the heart of the house,
But not into mine!"

"Noah Rondo is an outstanding personality. The guys who went to laugh at him, remained to laugh with him, and a right good laugh it was. Despite his years, he looked like old Charon, the boatman of Styx, a man of youthful vigor and autumnal green visage. His sense of humor keeps him youthful. His merriment was joyous, warm and friendly, indicating deep feeling and a sincere and honest heart. It was great to see a man of his age whose opinions have not jellied, whose mind has not lost its elasticity, and whose sympathies remain cheerful and undulled. Methinks he has not contracted the disease called Old Age.

"Johnnie Jones salutes him, and sends him this Turkish benediction:—May peace and prosperity go with him through this fickle world, may only the sweetest dreams disturb his nightly slumber, may his song birds never cease to carol and may his shadow never grow less."

Spec Fowler, of the Albany *Times-Union,* a long-time friend of Noey summed up Rondeau's career very aptly in a column dated Oct. 22, 1961:

"For three or four years Noah John appeared at Sportsmen's shows which in their own way attempted to bring the outdoors indoors. But it wasn't Noah's way of life. It disrupted his normal living; it was upsetting, heady and exhilarating. For being a hermit he became a national figure; for living alone in the woods he became famous. The career was not based upon a solid enough foundation; it collapsed after the public had seen its fill.

"So today filled with memories but not embittered Noah has lived out the past ten years in the mountains he loves. 'Would you go back?' he is asked. Again the probing of the beard, again the combing.

'I am a realist,' he says, 'I am 78. About 75 articles I had in my Cold River home are now in the Adirondack Museum at Blue Mountain Lake. I worked a short time at the new Whiteface Mountain Museum. I don't want to be a burden to taxpayers but a man has to live.

"Thus the anachronism of the day,—the civilized man pursuing education yet seeking primitive peace, the man who was independent but who today is dependent, the man who once used a double-bitted axe in the woods of northern New York but who today uses only a pencil for his "secret" diary, the man who once tried to be oblivious to the softness of civilization but who today must live on its strength."

During the last few years of his life Noey's health steadily deteriorated. His journals for that period contain frequent references to stomach and bowel disorders, sleepless nights and many trips to Dr. Spranz of AuSable Forks. In 1966 he was hospitalized for a month in Lake Placid; in March of 1967 he was again in the hospital, where his condition was diagnosed as an obstruction the size of a turkey's egg (as he described it in a letter to his sister-in-law). He survived the surgery and lingered for weeks between life and death before he finally died during the afternoon of August 24, 1967. He was buried in the North Elba Cemetery.

Since he had long since used up what little money he had earned during his brief period of relative prosperity, he had been living on welfare for many years. So Essex County paid most of his funeral expenses.

So far the only memorial erected to him has been the sign bearing his name which was put up by the Conservation Department on the site of the Cold River Hermitage. His wigwams have long since collapsed and the roof of the Town Hall has caved in. A few of his log chains are still there and one of his lanterns hangs trapped in a tree which has grown around the handle.

In late March of 1957 the Hall of Records and the Beauty Parlor wigwam were dismantled and moved to the Adirondack Museum at Blue Mountain Lake, where they are now on exhibit.

On display there are also some 75 of Noah's "artifacts" and other belongings which he sold to the Museum in 1958. Among these are his much-used rocking chair, which he made from the planks from a scow originally owned by the Santa Clara Lumber Co.; one of his bearskins, his favorite bow, fringed deerskin jacket, fishbasket made from a beaver pelt and quiver improvised from the neck skin of a buck.

Inside the wigwam there is a representative array of photographs featuring N.J.R. An old logging chain is suspended over an open fireplace and from it dangles the ancient coffee pot which never ran dry at Cold River.

So at Blue Mountain Lake the memory of the hermit-mayor is also being perpetuated by visible reminders of Hermitage days just as the signboard is making reasonably sure that he will be remembered at the site itself.

But besides these displays there exist still other private and public mementos of Rondeau in the form of a considerable number of tape recordings, newspaper and magazine articles and numerous letters to his many correspondents.

Supplementing all these for those people who knew Noah well are the reservoirs of his friends' personal memories. And, judging by the variety of names which keep recurring in the journals over the years, Noey must have made a deep and indelible impression on an impressively large number of people from nearly all the proverbial walks of life. Obviously, such a uniformly high opinion must have been both earned and deserved.

For those who know him only as a name the journal excerpts, letters, and poems which constitute the remainder of this book will hopefully serve as an acceptable and reasonably accurate introduction to a remarkable man who was known to many as Noah John Rondeau, Adirondack hermit.

THE RONDEAU JOURNALS

During most of the years that Rondeau lived at Cold River he kept a diary in which he recorded daily events, thoughts and observations. Since he was intensely interested in astronomy and meteorology, there are also many notations of that nature. Apparently he had started such a record as early as the summer of 1932 because among his possessions is a notebook which contains entries for the period between August 7th and September 11th of that year. These deal almost entirely with his activities as a guide and handyman for several summer residents at Corey's.

Unless the journals for the next five years have been lost, there is a gap in his personal records until 1937, when he was wintering at his Cold River hermitage. The entries for Jan. 1 and 2, 1937 refer to a bow and arrow hunt with Roy and Joan Hathaway, his perennial holiday season hosts at the Bartlett Carry Club. Noah also cites his Christmas gift of the oversized meerschaum pipe which visitors at Cold River frequently mentioned in later years.

These abbreviated entries, plus others dealing with writing letters and washing clothes, continue until Jan. 13th. From that point on the journals are not kept with any degree of regularity and those that do appear generally consist of only one or two lines—and these are in code. The 1938 journal is missing. Those for the next three years show frequent omissions, and the one for 1944 is either unaccounted for or possibly never kept. There follows an unbroken run until 1967, the year of Noah John's death. Toward the end they became a mixture of scrapbook and diary and include many pungent remarks about people and events.

It is noteworthy that during the late '40's and into the '50's, the diary notations show not only greater regularity and more extended entries but also a decreasing use of his exasperating code.

This code of his must certainly represent considerable ingenuity. Noah boasted that even the experts would not be able to decipher it. Seemingly composed of a wide variety of unrelated figures, at first glance it looks very much like the symbols seen on Indian wampum belts. While he never explained his cryptography to even his closest friends, the Hermit did say that in addition to symbols he used circles, squares, compass points and signs of the Zodiac in addition to a combination of intermixed French and English meteorological designations. A friend of Noah who considered himself to be an expert in the field gave up after a three-month try at decoding the hieroglyphics, which he declared bore a startling resemblance to the erratic footprints of an inebriated hen. Whatever the system, its hidden meanings will remain a challenging enigma until some more resourceful and patient person is willing to undertake the project.

Since the journals, particularly those kept during the Cold River period and his appearances at various sportsmen's shows, provide such an excellent index to his thoughts, moods, impressions and experiences, a typically characteristic sampling is therefore provided.

Although Noey kept a diary during the last eight months of his life, its present whereabouts is unknown. But, like the others, it should serve as a very reliable index to his varying moods and declining health—especially the latter. It is noteworthy that while much of his handwriting is surprisingly steady for a man over 80, there are many entries which are very shaky and indicate increasing infirmity. All in all they represent the best available key to the mind of a remarkable person.

In fairness to both Noah and the record it must be pointed out that this shared invasion of his privacy requires that the readers understand that the Hermit, like every other person of his age, lived mostly in the past.

Moreover, since those bygone years contained such a mixture of the pleasant and the unpleasant, it is not difficult to figure out why a hurt and sensitive man would show occasional outbursts of lingering bitterness and vindictiveness.

Nor should we lose sight of the fact that the Hermit had probably not foreseen that his diaries, which served as a therapeutic safety valve for his spells of emotional spontaneous combustion, would ever be made public.

Furthermore, since he sounded off so fully, frequently and forcefully in the journals, one wonders what could possibly have been left unsaid which required his resorting to code. Someday, someone who has infinite patience and a flair for that form of mental gymnastics may, as was done with the famous diaries of Samuel Pepys, satisfy both his and others' appreciable curiosity. Till then all we can do is wait and wonder, but in the meantime hope that the interval won't require a century-plus hiatus.

As a starter the cover of his 1945 journal bears these words: Fancy diary made at Cold River, by N. J. Rondeau, maker of fancy diaries. Wigwam smoke and Fly Specks a Specialty.

Jan. 1, 1945

Lest we forget, lest we forget
Snow and Winter are with us yet.
We still have Roosevelt (Roosterfelt)—
And we've got him for four years more
Unless the Devil should foreclose
The Devil is our only hope for riddance
Of this arrogant, Democratic imposition.

Feb. 2, 1945

Over 3 feet of hard-packed snow prevail over this mountainous region and it's a nice hardset, tough winter. Feeble sunshine through dense atmosphere. Mountains bluish, smoky as if insinuating a thaw.

Feb. 4, 1945 — Cold River

I read and write, cut wood and chop a chunk off Old Buck. I read Van Dyke's *Days Off*. At sundown hear barred owls hoot. Very cloudy and misty. I got civilization's complaint (cold).

March 27, 1945 — At Town Hall

I cut my hair, trim whiskers and give birds a lining for cradles. Summerlike sunshine, brown butterflies, Robins, Song Sparrow and a pair of ducks. Frogs first talk in Cold River mudhole. Elder leaves an inch long. Two deer parade by garden.

May 30, 1945

Rain last night; topography very wet. When I got up (8 a.m.) a great snow blizzard was in active descent and continued for an hour. Left no accumulation—just a specialty for Decoration Day.

June 1, 1945

Ice thicker than glass on water pail. I walk to Ampersand Park and put in night with Frank Blanchard.

June 30, 1945

Nice summer day with Dear Flies. Thank you June —come again.

July 12, 1945

A perfect summer day at Town Hall. Dr. and Mrs. Dittmar called. Nice trout picnic at Seward Pond.

Nov. 25, 1945

Just finished 24 mile walk to mail tag to American, weak-minded Blood and dishonest American Flesh (the Conservation Commission).

Jan. 1, 1946

Lest we forget, lest we forget
1945 is gone but the war debt

Is with us yet—is with us yet.
1945 took Roosevelt—took Roosevelt
Thanks—lest we forget, lest we forget
Another Roosevelt
Twil' be hard to get—hard to get

1946—All in Code

Jan. 1, 1947 Cold River Town Hall

Two feet of snow cover the ground
And too icy crust substantially bind
And it's seven score days to dandelions.
From wigwams—birch, maple, ash
From rivers—water, crystals of ice
From buck—3 pounds via two face axe
This is the ration card of N. J. R.

Jan. 2, 1947

A chick-a-dee bird tried my weasel trap—and it worked. I read Thoreau.

Jan. 3, 1947

The chick-a-dee Bird that got killed in the weasel trap yesterday is still dead, Mr. Burmaster. Two blue jays trapped in snow on wood at Poet's Maples.

Jan. 10, 1947

William Petty dropped note and package from Air Plane. I chopped frozen tail off Old Buck Deer in Wigwam. The bucktail soup was bully. The mountains are wonderful. I process buckskin leather. The Chick-a-dee Birds call at camp for Slam Bang. (stew)

Jan. 17, 1947

I silkwind and paint Arrow shafts. I eat Old Buck and Beans. No thanks to Big American business!

Feb. 9, 1947

I get wood for the night and write blunt lines about Conservation Commission.

Feb. 11, 1947

W. E. Petty drop letter and package from Air Plane —came near spoiling my snow.

Feb. 12, 1947

21 below zero Cold River. W. E. Petty arrive in helicopter. 4 men come and go one by one. (author's note: one was John Wingate) Pictures, Recorder, News Reels. 3 p.m. I fly over Ampersand Mountain. Over 200 wait for me at Saranac Lake Field. I talk with Mr. C. P. Seagers in N.Y.C. To Headquarters with W. E. Petty. Meet Mrs. Petty and daughter Marilyn.

Feb. 14, 1947

Saranac Lake at Mid-day I speak on Radio programme. I fletch arrows. I pack up to go to N.Y. city. 4 p.m. I board Colonial plane. 5:45 p.m. land at La Guardia Field N.Y.C. Reporters and photographers. To Grand Central Palace: Town Hall replica O.K. Broadcast 2 programs over W.O.R.

Feb. 15, 1947

John Rondeau and wife call on me at beginning of show. Grace Hudowalski and Leander Chadeayne call. I write autographs 5 hours and speak 4 hours to large crowds.

Feb. 16, 1947

At Sportsmen's show I write autographs all day (noon to 10 p.m.)

Feb. 17, 1947

N.Y.C. show: I speak to thousands and write autographs. Caller came from "We the People."

Feb. 18, 1947

Grand Central Palace: I see first live moose. Adolph G. Wiezel overtake me at Allen's Restaurant. Henry Burguiere of Norwood, N.J. call.

Feb. 19, 1947

Raccoons broke loose last night (from cages). Jay L.

Gregory and son—Dr. William B. Gregory called, having come from Binghamton by Air Line. I answer questions and write autographs.

Feb. 20, 1947

At show: Harry Johnson of Lewis called, so did John St. Dennis of Elizabethtown. I broadcast for Mr. St. George, 11 p.m. 12 p.m. NightClub of our own—Chipman, Keeting, Capt. Lampfort and Ernest Thatcher all call.

Feb. 21, 1947

At show: Long talk (evolution) with lady. Madden Gift Shop give me 3 ducks. Mr. St. George give me 2 boxes of Cartridges. Exhibit bring me Ice Cream. Ed and Grace Hudowalski and E. A. Harmes call.

Feb. 23, 1947

Last day of show. 10:30 I broadcast "We the People."

Feb. 24, 1947

New York city quite cloudy. Storm raging in Adk. Mts. 2 p.m. I board Colonial Plane NC21751. Plane stop at Glens Falls, I get off at Burlington, Vt. I hug little girl for picture. Photo with 70 year old C. F. Cleveland. I take train to Plattsburgh. Arrive at Conservation Commission's Headquarters in Lake Clear 10 p.m.

Feb. 26, 1947

At Conservation Commission Headquarters at Saranac Inn. I rest, sleep and eat then write 8 letters. I write "my report" of Sportsmen's Show to Essex County Republican.

Feb. 27, 1947

I'm getting ready to go to Albany tomorrow.

Feb. 28, 1947

Friday, winter weather. To Albany—Toomey drive conservation car. High snow banks, decked conifer trees.

Mar. 1, 1947

Albany, I work at Sportsmen's Show. I cut ribbon at opening.

Mar. 3, 1947

Albany. 2 p.m. making Broadcast Record. 5 to 11 on duty at Show. 7 p.m. listen to record made today. 11:45 p.m. I find D. H. Toomey dead, in room on 11th floor of Hotel Ten Eyck.

At show a Pale Face in Salvation Army Bonnet wants to know: "What are you going to do with John 3:16?"

Mar. 4, 1947

Albany Show. I spend forenoon with Clayt Seagers. 32 senators call. I have 3 manhattans. I see myself (Cold River reel).

Mar. 13, 1947

At Gloversville. I made two speeches each 30 minutes with Mr. Jeremiah—speaking between my two subjects "A Year with a Hermit" and "Nine Days at New York City Sportsmen's Show."

Mar. 15, 1947

Buffalo Sportsmen's Show. Speech to Buffalo crowd "How I became a Hermit."

Mar. 16, 1947

Buffalo—show is on: A family of 4 Esquimos called. Good diving floppers.Ski jumper. And *good* trained seal.

April 5, 1947

Rochester Sportsmen's Show opens at Armory. Radio broadcast 6:30.

April 27, 1947

Burnt Hills Sportsmen's Show last 2 days. Cloudy, breezy, 2 glimpses sunshine, 2 very light showers and 1 handful snow flakes.

May 1, 1947

I go shopping at Saranac Lake, Starks, Woolworth, Grays, Drutz and Enterprise. Evening I go to Fish and Game club with W. E. Petty and I speak to members 50 minutes—subjects—City Belles, Trail Full of Old Maids. The Hermit was made Honorary member of Saranac Lake Fish and Game Club.

May 3, 1947

New York city. I put in 3 hours at C.B.S. Had nice visit at Studio with Old timers I met there last February. I put in 3 hours in Studio No. 3 on 21st floor for "We the People" on C.B.S. corner 52nd-Madison.

May 10th, 1947

Drive to Loon Lake with Putman. Nice buildings, much cobble stone work. Nice hills, nice drive and nice greening fields trimmed with Robins.

May 18, 1947

Saranac Inn. I pack "Paul Delaire" Box and apply anti Insect powder. I pack 16 packages to send on Aerial flight to Cold River.

May 20, 1947

Good evening visit with Mr. and Mrs. Avery Rockefeller and Frank Blanchard at Ampersand Park.

May 21, 1947

Ampersand Park to Cold River. To wash out near Ward Creek Leanto with Frank Blanchard. Then I walk to Cold River. Someone broke Town Hall lock. Little water Frogs after dormant winter, cuddle in mud under sloughs of water have their Pianos in tune.

May 25, 1947

A May Day. It is Vernal May's happy Spring Time
The Mother Does have spotted Fawns
With Buds the Hills are Purple Brown
And a Robin's nesting in my Wigwam.

May 28, 1947

At Cold River Wigwams. I work in Garden, play violin and eat fish.

June 1, 1947

This is first June Day in 11 months, and not much different from Yesterday the last of May.

June 6, 1947

Donald Latimer called and brought mail. We test Dr. Latimer's Scotch.

June 13, 1947

This morning: Fresh Deer Track in Mrs. Rondeau's Kitchenette. Young Robins leave Wigwam Nest. Big deer in Buck Slough at Dusk. Bunchberry blossoms at Standard Best. I haul Balsam Boughs to make fancy bed.

June 18, 1947

At mid day Wm. Petty called. And he brought my mail and we had a Mountain Lunch; and the hundred minute talk like the June Day needs no Professor's Polish.

June 21, 1947

Clear 2 miles of trail towards Lake Placid. Put up for night with Ranger Quigley at mouth of Moose Creek.

June 23, 1947

Air plane drop 4 packages at Cold River Town Hall. Lash party help to pick up. Just before dusk air plane return and drop 4 more packages—scatter photos, writing paper and .22 caliber cartridges in Sand Pit. Again I chase more tin cans.

July 3, 1947

Rouses Point. Artist S. Y. Willick sketches the Hermit, N. J. Rondeau. Good Show at Rouses Point.

July 5, 1947

I pose for 4 portraits by S. Y. Willick. Mid-night I draw ticket for winning Pontiac car (from drum).

July 10, 1947

At Moose Creek lean-to says Bill Petty—"Your friend Earle Vosburgh had heart trouble."

July 17, 1947

Cold River. Two Raccoons came to camp last night. They investigate—knock dishes off table and grease their mustaches with Boot Grease.

Noey in fancy Cold River regalia. Photo by Ed Hudowalski.

Composite of Rondeau and his Wigwam City. Photo courtesy of N.Y. State Conservation Department.

The violin virtuoso of Cold River City. Dittmar photo.

Troy 46ers in early 1940. Left to right, front row: Erna Austin, Janet Ryder Brown; middle row: Charles Horn, William Lance, Mary Devin Spence, Clarence Craver, Edward Hudowalski; rear row: Dorothy Ryder Brown, Ralph Iler, Frank Johnston, Margery Ludlow, Joseph Warnock, Grace L. Hudowalski.

Greetings, folks, states N.J.R. Photo by Ditt Dittmar.

"Robin" Rondeau and Jay L. Gregory of Binghamton.
Photo by Dr. William Gregory.

N. J. Rondeau contemplating a trout dinner. Photo by E. A. Harmes, June, 1946.

N. J. Rondeau putting fish in menu, June, 1946. Charles Wright photo.

Noah John Rondeau
Adirondack Hermit

Autograph

Dr. and Mrs. William L. Gregory, 1938. Both died in crash of their private plane near Lima, Ohio, in 1948.

Paganini and his enthralled listener — Mary Dittmar. Dittmar photo.

Noah John and home-made telescope.

Versatile Hermit and friend, Ranger Orvil Betters.

July 24, 1947

I shoot Red Squirrel off Pyramid of Giza. (one of wigwams).

July 31, 1947

A nice summer day at Tupper Lake. Have Molar extracted by Dr. Leland Foote, Call at Tavern. Meet Philadelphia party (Kate Smith). Ride to Corey's P.O. with Kate Smith Party.

Aug. 10, 1947

Nasturtiums are at glorious best. Humming birds call to please the flowers.

Aug. 16, 1947

Shattuck Clearing, Plumley Camp. I wish to hop off. Stormy weather prevents aerial flight. I stay—visit with guests—join evening party. Munch, sip, laugh and talk to two o'clock next a.m.

Aug. 17, 1947

I do a big lot of sleeping—after the night before.

Sept. 6, 1947

Nice summer day at Cold River Town Hall. I assemble relics to take out. Fresh deer tracks within four feet of my bed. I paint clouds on old oil painting.

Sept. 10, 1947

Francis Quigley carry load to Moose Creek for me. And I do two miles of trail for him. Later I do Cold River laundry.

Sept. 12, 1947

Quigley and Rutledge call and I go with them to Moose Creek. We carry 3 loads out—Rocking Chair, etc.

Sept. 17, 1947

Moose Creek and Saranac Inn Station. Breakfast with F. G. Quigley, dinner at Tom Peckham's, supper at Conservation Commission headquarters.

Sept. 25, 1947

Quite cloudy, stingy sun shine near Saranac Inn Station. White pines never so loaded with cones. Autumn colors coming on slow. Harvest of apples, squash, corn and pumpkins renew memories of their habitat in gone by years.

Oct. 4, 1947

Marilyn Petty hid my square. Have a good notion to put her in Tom Derby's cement mixer. I build second strong box and touch up mountain on replica curtain.

Nov. 21, 1947

Ampersand Park—Big Dam (Cold River) see 2 deer at east end of Park. A 10 pointer hang at Ward Brook Leanto. From Mountain Pond to camp 12 Bear tracks —one bear.

Dec. 31, 1947

At Saranac Lake 9 a.m. I call on Bill Carson and at Commo's Studio. 10 a.m. I meet Carnival Parade at Veteran's Club. 1:40 Parade start. 4 p.m. move Town Hall replica to Saranac Hotel second floor. Today: Parade was very good, crowd was extra good.

Jan. 3, 1948

I write autographs at Hotel Saranac. Meet Senator and Mrs. William A. Hannan of West Virginia. At 11 p.m. I crown Winter King and Queen (Robert Sullivan and Jean Keating).

Jan. 9, 1948

I pose for artists at Hotel Alpine (Saranac Lake). I paint on Saranac Scene. I paint first portrait.

Jan. 13, 1948

Autograph 100 autographs. Get letter from Campbell—Fairbanks about Boston Sportsmen's Show. 7-10 p.m. I pose for 16 artists at Hotel Alpine.

Jan. 23, 1948

6 p.m. Board bus for Hotel Marcy (Lake Placid). Supper with Mr. Enoch Squires. Address guests in Fire Place room. In Blue Room contract with Mrs. Rideout

(lady aerial pilot) to become aerial pilot next summer. Midnight I do artistic dance with Rose Madden in Blue Room.

Feb. 1, 1948

I have civilization's distemper (common cold).

Mar. 29, 1948

Utica. On duty at Sport Show from noon to 11 p.m. I read three poems at three shows: "To a Baby," "Adirondack Winter," and "Living Among Hills." In morning call on Fashionable Clothiers, 103 Oriskany St.

Mar. 30, 1948

On duty at Sport Show. Three minute speech on "Fishing," four minute on "Bear Eat Me Up," five minute on "Hatchet Burnt Up." At 5 p.m. broadcast for WGAT.

April 10, 1948

Deposit and Binghamton. Call on Edward A. Harmes —call at Editorial Office. Grass is greening, early flowers blooming, leaves are peeking.

April 12, 1948

One p.m. to Luzerne Central School. Address the students 55 minutes on Natural History, Mountains, Vallies, etc. Franklin D. Roosevelt died 1945.

April 15, 1948

83 years ago today Abraham Lincoln died—and he's been dead ever since.

Apr. 19, 1948

I overhaul my Show Outfit. Mend bed and Rocking Chair. Robins laugh, whisper and make love in Spring Time ground.

May 22, 1948

Saranac Lake—Ampersand Park. Cold River groceries from William Mullen. Veteran poppy from Miss Curr. Ride to Corey's with Lawyer Cantwell, Jr. Walk to Ampersand West Gate. Met Mr. and Mrs. Avery

Rockefeller. Supper and lodge with Frank Blanchard at West Gate.

May 25, 1948

At Cold River. I work in Garden. Deer chase me into camp. I cut poles, set tripod and hang 3 caldrons of flowers.

May 30, 1948

Cold River. I climb Couchsachraga. Then fish Seward Pond. Blue Grass bloom. First Scarlet Tanager Scream.

June 5, 1948

Leave Saranac Lake with Prof. J. Potter. Drive most beautiful among mountains dressed in tender vernal green—lilacs good. Called at Adirondack House, Long Lake. Congenial spirit—beautiful. 9 p.m. New Hartford. 11 p.m. Ithaca. 11:30 Barton Scout Camp, Cayuga Lake. Next evening I speak 70 minutes to about 200 people.

July 1, 1948

At Cold River Wigwams. Good morning, July. Search for packages dropped by Air Plane last night. Found one in Big Eddy. Roy Lash tried to run Spotted Fawn over me—missed by 10 feet. I put away groceries all day.

July 19, 1948

Fresh deer tracks in Beauty Parlor and Mrs. Rondeau's Kitchenette within four feet of my bed. Am reading "Lin Yutang." Deer also trim pansys in two iron caldrons. Fair-sized buck deer eat noodle soup in Beauty Parlor.

Aug. 31, 1948

I see 8 point buck and a Doe. They are in blue coat. They frolic chase over grassy Pond bottom. Finally they come near running over me. They bolt—look me over for 2 minutes—then gallop to camp and make tracks in Fireplace before I pull into Camp. I collect Pearly Everlasting and investigate View Point to paint North Mountains of Seward Range. In medium Evening Dusk moon stand on Panther Peak.

Sept. 24, 1948

Drive 16 miles north of Plattsburgh with Mr. Byrne to look over fossiliferous Rocks on Shore of Lake Champlain. Sundown picnic at Cumberland Point. At 8 p.m. I speak to 200 people. At 10 o'clock next day a.m. on Radio WMFF.

Oct. 31, 1948

I have dinner with three New York city hunters at Big Eddy. Spend pleasant afternoon with Lucius Russell (Ranger at Shattuck's Clearing). Later on bury carrots and rutabagas in garden. Next day I consider my riches and arrange to close Town Hall for winter.

Nov. 14, 1948

From Blanchard's at Ampersand Park went to Mountain Pond with 4 men and a truck and we carry 600 pounds from Cold River City.

Nov. 15, 1948

I ride with Frank Blanchard to Ward Creek Bridge. Go to rugged Notch between Peche's Lumber Camp and Ouluska Pass. Last (?) lunch at Boulder Basin? Returning I picked up Mattock I hid ten years ago. Next day down North Side of Peek-a-Boo Hill to 1915 Trap Line. See Sun set over White Lily Pond.

Dec. 23, 1948

At Saranac Lake. 4 inches of snow cover the ground. Trees and roofs are in Christmas shine. And from the Zenith Flakes of Snow have put a loaf on every Post. Garry McCalvin, 2 years old, makes his Old Mother and Hermit join him in Santa Klaus Dance before Morning Twilight.

Saranac Lake and Lake Clear. Set up Cold River Town Hall on Winter Sleigh for Carnival Parade.

Dec. 27, 1948

10 a.m. Carnival Parade from Veteran's Memorial Club House to Riverside Park. Good parade, good crowd. I

play Violin in front of Town Hall and put it on stage in Saranac Town Hall. 6-9 supper with Lions at Hotel Saranac. I put on 15 minute speech. Later I spend 4 hours writing autographs for Teen Agers.

Jan. 4, 1949

7 to 10 p.m. First ever—Sportsmen's Show at Saranac Lake.

Jan. 7, 1949

I knock down Replica of Cold River City (Wigwam, Town Hall, Mountains and Sky). I make a King's staff and a Queen's Bouquet. I attend a Ball at Hotel Saranac.

11 o'clock: I crown King and Queen at Hotel Saranac.

Jan. 27, 1949

I engage Roy Bomyea to transfer my Exhibit to Boston. (for Sportsmen's Show).

7 p.m. Miss Millicent Pierce meet me at Alpine Hotel and take me to Trudeau. I speak to splendid Audience at Trudeau Recreation Hall. We have doughnuts and coffee. I sell photographs.

Feb. 2, 1949

At Boston, Mass. Snowed 2 inches—slushy. I trim Replica to finish at Mechanic's Building. 1:15 to 1:45 On the air with Ken and Carolan—Yankee Network Programme at 21 Brookline Ave.

5 Raccoons and 1 eagle arrive next to my Exhibit. Boston is doing itself proud with Sportsmen's Show setup.

Feb. 3, 1949

Saturday. Cloudy and cool. At Boston Mass., Sportsmen's Show. On duty at my exhibit. I follow up a woman and take a Photo away from Her—after she stold it.

Feb. 21, 1949

Saranac Lake. After cool night sun rise catch twirling, crystal, celestial show and reveals colors like Zodiac sifting Rain Bow Dust below. I call at P.O. among floating crystal.

Feb. 22, 1949

Very cloudy, cool, evening rain. I call at P.O. Gladys says "No Mail." N.J.R. says "Nobody loves us." Gladys: "To hell with them."

March 31, 1949

At Tahawus: I put final touches on Exhibit for show. At 10 o'clock I go with Charles Begor to Upper "Iron Works" along Lake Sanford. A Stone Furnace Building closed operations about 1857-58. Old Red Building (Bank) of long ago—first Bank north of Albany.

Tahawus: 11,000 acres. First Steel made in U. S. A. 450 men work at Tahawus (60 in mine). Largest Titanium Metal Mine in World.

1 o'clock: Sportsmen's Show begin. On duty 10 hours. Visitors: Ed. Keat, John Longware, Bill E. Petty (wants his hat autographed).

April 9, 1949

AuSable Forks—Black Brook. Quite cool and cloudy. Breakfast at Halsey Payro's. Walk to Haywood Farm. Ride to Black Brook with Chester Rondeau. Have supper.

8 o'clock to William Rondeau's. Lodge for night. Another supper—then a Dandy Deer and Bear Hunt that lasted passed Mid-night.

April 11, 1949

Tom McCasland's big Rooster attack me at Mastoid Ledge and if it had not been for my Palmer Hill cane I would have been licked.

April 12, 1949

Cool today, Perfect Sun. At McCasland Farm. I take Beauty Walk about the Farm.

I plant over 100 Spruce Seeds and as I plant Seeds by the Barn, the Full Moon rises over the Mountain; and within 2 degrees of Earth's Shadow—approaching Lunar Eclipse.

The Lunar Eclipse was well displayed, as Black Eclipse, in Cloudless Sky; plus Aurora borealis during Totality.

April 27, 1949

Sunshine, clouds and showers. Saranac Lake and Ampersand. 5 a.m. Ride to Corey's with Phillip McCalvin. Walk to 2nd Gate. Ride to Ampersand Pond with Blanchard—Martins and Chase. Camps all broken by Bear.

Spring music is here: Night Hawks, Robins, Northern Flickers, Juncos, Blue Jays and Water Birds.

May 1, 1949

Sunshine morning: P.M. cloudy. 6 o'clock—snow squall.

I find Ham, Bacon and Salt Pork near Big Eddy—also a Bag of Potatoes. I split 8 loaves of Rye Bread and dry them in the Sun. *Hard Tacks* for an Old Man without any Sons.

May 3, 1949

High water after rain today—perfect sunshine at Cold River Town Hall. I transplant Fox Gloves, Pansies and Daisies—also Tiger Lilies and Cat-Nip.

First Bluets bloom on Cold River Bank—first white violets and trailing Arbutus. First Snake. A pair of Red Tail Hawks soar and whistle.

Sun Down: It's been a wonderful Vernal Day, calm and sunshine. I saw Black Cherry leaves greening in the hours of sunshine.

May 4-8, 1949

Sunshine and clouds—nice day at Cold River.

First Owl Hoot—try his vocabulary. I plant Potatoes, Pansies and Nasturtiums. First Purple Violet and Gold Thread Bloom.

First Painted Trillium Blossoms. 1st Belted Kingfisher arrive at Cold River Dam. 1st shad and sweet alder bloom.

May 12, 1949

Slight breeze, clouds and sunshine at Cold River. At midday a Deer in Buck Slough.

I read from end to end. "The Religion of Dr. Trudeau," by James Arthur Miller. First pair of Blue Birds at the Dam.

May 15, 1949

Ice on water in pail today. Perfect sun and calm.

3 fishermen go home to Plattsburg, after a night in the Hall of Records. Shad blossom Petals are falling. First Gold Finch. Last night something took a 9 inch trout and 2 fish heads from an earthen jar.

May 17-19, 1949

I paint "Town Hall" on piece of blue overalls.

In deep shade of evening dusk—a deer waltz by the Wigwam called "Rotten Gut." I whittle and shape a deer-rubbed maple cane.

First Little Black Fly bit the Mayor. Blue Berries and Elder Bushes are blooming. Spring time at Cold River Wigwam; fried trout and boiled dandelions.

First Humming Bird come to my Town Hall Door and buzz his propellers like Humming Birds years before.

May 25, 1949

Shower last night. Today cold, cloudy, breezy; 11 o'clock—5 minutes snow storm small granules hit ground, hop, roll, stop 2 seconds as snow, then liquidize.

I sit on my fancy bed in my Town Hall and watch the Dance of the Snow. 5 p.m. Three whitish planes go like strange birds a few degrees north of east. 7 p.m. Deer cross east end of Buck Slough. 11 p.m. Raccoon call at Town Hall and stand up on hind feet to gaze at Flash Light.

June 4, 1949

A happy long day at Scout Camp Ground camporee, 11 miles from Ithaca. 9 p.m. I speak for an hour at Scout's Camp Fire.

1,000,022 Grass Hoppers.

Big Bear died about 1920 and he's been dead ever since.

June 11, 1949

Perfect sunshine continues at Saranac Lake-Ampersand Pond.

I write 2 letters—3 post cards. Call at Express Office.

Firemen continue to raise hell. Many Bands and Fire Trucks in P.M. Parade. Parade was good enough to set beautiful if the Brainless Fools had not raised hell for 3 days before parade started.

7 p.m. I ride to Ampersand Pond with Frank Blanchard.

June 13, 1949

Very hot sun—few clouds at Cold River Town Hall. At Sunrise Deer blow at Big Dam. P.M. Mother Duck and 7 babies at Big Dam. I sew canvas and canopy 2 wigwams.

The dear little Midges are hot footed.

June 24, 1949

Hot sun—clouds and Deer Flies at Cold River Town Hall. 5 a.m. Big Red Doe at Beauty Parlor. 9 to 10 a.m. The tame doe stays near Beauty Parlor.

Tall Meadow Rue is in blossom.

4 Adirondackers—(Hogue, Dodge and two Dittmars) arrive from Ausable Forks. Big Packs—Lame Backs. A Swim—Supper. Campfire, Photographs—Violin.

In deepest shade of dusk and a buck deer came to Camp Fire; made two trips from Beauty Parlor to Pyramid of Giza: finally he come up 12 feet from glowing camp fire and 5 people. For 5 minutes strain eyes to see who in hell came from Ausable Forks, while I play Violin.

June 25, 1949

Cloudy and showers and pesky flies at Cold River City.

9 a.m. breakfast; 12 noon at Seward Pond. 3 p.m. back to camp. Luncheon—Beauty nap.

Splendid supper. Another Glowing camp fire. More Violin Harmony. A lot of talk about anything.

July 4, 1949

Peace—Beauty—Tranquility at Cold River City. Hurrah, Fourth of July. Let fools celebrate theory of Independence and tolerate bondage;—But give me the day, alone, mountains, even with deer flies.

July 6, 1949

I make a mattock handle. I carry Stones to mark Place of Hermit Dust, 5 large flat stones and about 2,000 pebbles.

4 mice trapped in Town Hall. First ripe Blueberries.

July 10, 1949

Much rain last night. Today cool breeze, clouds, sunshine.

I chose 15 stones from Cold River's water way, on which to engrave my name to mark a Place for Dust's Relay.

7 p.m. A Buck Deer at foot of Golden Stairs—later at west wigwam—then across Potato Patch and once and a half around Beauty Parlor; then through brush along Sand Pit (15 minute parade).

10:30 p.m. A Raccoon under table Bench and one on top of Mrs. Rondeau's Kitchenette—as Jupiter stand 13 degrees over Couchsachraga and the Full Moon exactly between (in Capricornus).

July 11-15, 1949

8 a.m. Old Doe near Rotten-Gut Wigwam.

10 a.m. Lucius Russell and Edward Lance call. I read my mail.

10 p.m. Deer eyes at 2,000 Pebbles Ash Ground . . .

I take beauty walk about my city. Spirea is beginning to blossom. 10 p.m. A Raccoon push me off the bench so he can climb on the Table . . .

Perfect summer weather at Cold River Town Hall. I write 3 letters.

4 p.m. An Old Doe come about 9 paces from where I write and get Salt while bulging her black eyes at me.

10 p.m. The Raccoon call; when I stepped out, he was surprised as he was only a yard from me; Stood on hind feet and growled at me. It seem he will soon come in Town Hall and box my ears.

July 17, 1949

The dear little Deer Flies are with us yet. 10 p.m. Deer eyes at Ash Ground.

July 22, 1949

Very cloudy—light showers. Raccoon at corn last night. Mouse in trap.

A hand full of Raspberries at Noah's Grave (Ash Ground). Perennial Sweet Peas are at standard best. I cremate 3 potato bugs.

Aug. 1, 1949

A perfect August summer day, in perfect solitude of Cold River Hermitage. After Rain, Morning as cool as a Cucumber on the vine, under the leaves. And as calm as Vacuum where a Feather moves an inch in a century.

Aug. 7, 1949

Raccoon and Deer make tracks 6 feet from my bed last night.

Peter Stone and Dad from Wilmington, Del., climb Couchsachraga.

Aug. 8, 1949

A hot summer day at Cold River City. 2 mice tried my traps to see if they work. They did!

First cricket utters his squeaks.

51 years ago today—ran away from home. Flew the coop in 1898.

Sept. 22, 1949

Rain last night. Today Cloudy a.m. P.M.—sunshine.

I plant 700 perennial sweet peas at my Ashes Ground. While working Ashes Ground found socket with point for spick pole.

Mice raise hell at night. The river is high.

Sept. 24, 1949

Autum colors getting good. I lay Flat Stones at Ashes Ground.

(author's note—N.J.R. comment re end of Daylight saving time): My watch don't need setting back. It's as near Standard Time as unconstant Sun and erroneous Calendar permits; and "my watch" is never set, to a Democrat's little 6 o'clock.

Sept. 25, 1949

I dig a 200 pound Boulder out of Path and put it on north end of Pebble Tray against Permanent Boulder on my Ashes Ground.

Sept. 29, 1949

Rain last night. Today very cloudy. At day break a Bear utters his notes. I transplant 32 Spruce trees to my Ashes Ground.

Oct. 8, 1949

Mild, cloudy, light showers. I transplanted 300 Fox Gloves among Spruce Trees squaring my Ash Tray. I put big Sod in front of Ash Tray.

Oct. 9, 1949

I do artistic work on my Ash Tray. I finish arrangement of name stones. (15): "NOAH JOHN RONDEAU."

Oct. 17, 1949

Ice on water pail—white briars. Today: Perfect October Sun at Cold River.

This is October time. Nights put ice on water and blanche the fields to whitish gray. Then sunshine vaporizes the roof and get summer warm by noon day.

A Buck rub Horns on Black Cherry Tree 75 feet from Town Hall Door.

I sit on Browning Grass near the Flow and watch the colors come and go. I walk to Belly Ache Swamp.

Nov. 13, 1949

Very cloudy, wind, showers, cold. At Chattock Clearing. I carry Bill Petty's Basket to Jack Ass Gate. I stay at Big Horn Camp most of the day.

Nov. 16, 1949

Ice last night. Today: cloudy, cold. Mountain tops are white.

10 a.m. 3 hunters call—from Whiteman camp.

I hunt 3 legged Swamp. 3 to 4 p.m. I watch at Mouth of Seward Brook. Saw a Big Buck at Seward Brook Bridge.

Nov. 21, 1949

10 a.m. leaving Cold River. Noon: at Mountain Pond; 2 p.m. Ward Creek; 5 p.m. Ampersand Pond. Saw a deer in Park. 10 inches Snow on height of Land.

Nov.26, 1949

Cloudy and cold at Saranac Lake. I write Tahawus Sportsmen's Show.

Evening: I tune up dee fiddle and fiddle stick the Devil's Dream until dee Devil had a Night Mare.

Dec. 2, 1949

New York City. International Theatre N.B.C. "We The People" Television. Rehearsals at 3:15 and 6:30 Broadcast 8:30 to 9:30 p.m.

Dec. 13, 1949

At Saranac Lake. I call at 14 Academy Street. Confab with Dick Smith, Anna Rice, Frank Baker and Mrs. Vosburg and Mrs. Bray.

2 o'clock I attend Rites for Charles Middlebrook Palmer (who died Saturday at age 93) at St. Lukes Church.

Scribbler's Note: I guide Irving S. Cobb in Palmer's Party July 6, 1923.

Dec. 17, 1949

Saranac Lake. Herman Bova from Ogdensburg call and leave a gallon of wine.

Anna Pettnato came to 4 Alpine Terrace and played pinochle. We drank the gallon of wine.

Jan. 24, 1950

Saranac Lake. I call on Samuel Edleberg and go with him to Rotary Club as his Guest for dinner. I won a Rotary Wheel.

Feb. 8, 1950

Last night: 24 degrees below zero.

I purchase a Pot of live Flowers for a Queen; and I trim 2 canes.

7:30 p.m. I crown King and Queen.

Feb. 11, 1950

Saranac Lake. Mild, cloudy. One o'clock: Carnival Parade start from New York Central Depot and on to Riverside Park. I go on parade with Fish and Game Club with Violin.

March 2, 1950

At Fish and Game Club won a prize in Liar's Club. Home with Bob Liddie.

Mar. 25-26, 1950

At Marathon, N. Y. I entertain at 3 stores six hours greeting customers. Several people call at Holmes' to see Hermit. I go with Mr. and Mrs. Holmes for car ride in beautiful vallies among beautiful hills.

Back home Mrs. Holmes play piano, Mr. Holmes play a Saw—I play Violin. Several people call. Good visit, Happy Day at Marathon.

2 o'clock to Bainbridge with H. V. Holmes. Supper for 258 at 7:30. Reset for 30 more; then about 10 brief speakers. 9:30 to 11:05 I give 75 minutes lecture on Hermit life and Hermit Debut.

April 1, 1950

At Tahawus Sportsmen's Show—10 a.m. to 10 p.m. Ditts (Mary, David and Ditt), Ed Worthington, Johnny Longware, Bob Liddie—Mrs., Mr. Bert. I met many people. Good Show, good crowd—good weather.

May 3, 1950

Perfect warm sunshine. Saranac Lake. I call on Bill Betters at Town Hall.

I call on Peter Lamoy—bargain for a piece of Ground.

May 13, 1950

I have Arthur Willett transfer 2 loads of Cold River City Replica from Conservation Commission Headquarters to Eklunds' at Coreys. Afternoon Philip McCalvin helped me to set up—"Cold River Town Hall."

May 25, 1950

At Corey's, N. Y. I make Ridge stick for Tent. Karl Eklund bring me Pansy Plants from Saranac and I plant them. I take down Eklund Tent and set up my new Tent.

P.M. committee from St. Regis Falls call to plan for my Exhibit at their American Legion Sportsmen's Show, May 28-29th.

June 6, 1950

First Deer Fly bite. The Dear, little Deer Flies.

July 2, 1950

Coreys. N. Y. Callers: Roy Snyder, Billy Burger. Daniel Emmett arrive from Canada.

July 14, 1950

Coreys, N. Y. Callers: Kate Smith Party.

I kill a chipmonk with an arrow. First nastortium blossom.

Karl Eklund go to hospital.

Aug. 3, 1950

Cloudy morning then sunshine. 1 to 3 cloud burst flood the Cold River Town Hall at Coreys.

I gether a batch of potato bugs, not having time to make a chowder, I cremate.

Callers: Eugene Freeman, Eklund Boarders.

Aug. 5, 1950

8 a.m. I ride with Mr. Julian J. Reiss to Santa Claus City at North Pole, in White Face Mountain. The ride is beautiful.

I put on Santa Claus uniform and I'm Santa Claus for 9 hours. I greet thousands. A thousand cameras shot at me. I hold up hundreds of little tots for pictures.

Aug. 10, 1950

Nice summer day at Coreys. I take down Wigwam and Archery Target; and make ready to move to Santa Claus city at North Pole. I call on Dan Emmett.

Aug. 13, 1950

A perfect day at Santa Claus City, North Pole, N. Y.

I autograph and sell photos. I do my own cooking and get along very good in a crowd of 14,000 for the day.

Aug. 21, 1950

At Santa Claus City I do the Roll of Santa 8½ hours.

An American Thief took the Horns off my white deer skin today, and he got away with them; he wants a relic souvenir to hang on his wall to remind him that he is a Thief.

Oct. 9-11, 1950

North Pole, N. Y. I am Santa Claus all day. Today it's Thanksgiving Day in Canada. Many Canadians call at "North Pole." 2 o'clock: 63 Canadian Geese fly North West.

Oct. 31, 1950

Perfect sunshine, like summer day without bugs. With plenty of help I take down Wigwam—Town Hall and move to Lake Clear and Saranac Lake.

I saw a Rough Grouse on White Face Mountain Highway. The ride from North Pole to Lake Clear was most perfect, calm, warm and clear.

Nov. 1, 1950

Lucius Russell kill a bear (a very large bear).

Nov. 6, 1950

Saranac Lake. I buy and pack a multiplicity of items to take to Cold River Hunting and trapping. Harold Rightmyer of Ithaca shoot a Bobcat today at Cold River.

Nov. 7, 1950

Nice Sunshine—Saranac Lake—Chattock Clearing.

I pick up groceries at Bill Mullen's, personal items at 4 Alpine Terrace and snow shoes at Lake Clear. Then I stall items with Helm Bros. (flyers) at Long Lake. Then I fly to Plumley's—coffee, cookies and gossip with Ladies in kitchen. Then walk to Chattock Clearing—I find Lucius Russell and Rev. Morgan skinning a Bear.

Nov. 8-11, 1950

Chattock—Big Dam. Up at 4:30—Breakfast at Dawn. I go and skin a bear's head and salt the hide. And then walk 7 miles up Old River Trail. A Bob cat hang on pine limb at Rightmyer. 2 large bucks hang Camp Seward. I see a large deer in Cold River at mouth of Seward Brook.

At Cold River Town Hall. Big Dam. I clean camp—make new bed .... I drive out mice and set a trap. I look over my city streets—Cold River.

I boil bear's head. I pick up fallen Wigwam. I wait for Air Plane to bring supplies—no come.

I see doe and fawn south of Big Dam.

Cub plane, 2 trips, from Long Lake and bring supplies. I find Pick Axe near 9 foot boat under boulder.

Nov. 14, 1950

At Cold River, mild and cloudy.

9 a.m. I shoot from Town Hall Door and kill a 12 point Adirondack Buck. The last 3 years I saw the buck about 100 times near camp, and recorded him a score of times in my Diaries. I knew 9 of his beds . . . . . .Today two bullets took him almost instantly—at standard best.

Nov. 15, 1950

Very cloudy—mild temperature at Town Hall, Cold River.

I skin a Deer's head and neck. I boil a can of Slam Bang. I prepare American Fool Tags to compare with American Fool Law.

Nov. 25, 1950

Cold River—Ampersand Pond. Cloudy and fierce wind. Snow all gone.

I recanvas Town Hall roof where wind raise hell. I find 1 gallon glass jug full of sugar hid since 1934.

I walk 8 miles to Donkey Lodge. 4 to 7 p.m. Stop with Marcellus Hunters. 7 p.m. to Ampersand Pond with Frank Blanchard . . . . . . Hunting Season close.

Dec. 13, 1950

8 inches of snow cover the ground. Today calm and cool at Saranac Lake. I have civilization's distemper, that people call "a cold." I'm taking Bromo Quinine.

Dec. 24, 1950

At Saranac Lake. I get agreement from Campbell-Fairbanks for New York Sportsmen's Show.

Feb. 10, 1951

At Saranac Lake, I take down Remington Rifle and pack for launching for N.Y.C. I sew very cute stitches of

Red Yarn on my Hermit Vest. 10:30 at Carnival Parade: Tom Fink and Natalie Bombard crowned King and Queen by Mayor Alton Anderson. Later I do fancy stitches of Red Yarn on my Exhibit Pantaloons.

Feb. 18, 1951

At Grand Central Palace, N. Y. C. Sportsmen's Show 3 p.m. An American that look like a Man stole a photograph from me. Reminder: Be strictly careful about Photograph's at Sportsmen's Shows. Was not "strict" enough today.

Feb. 19, 1951

12:30 on Radio and Television. Next day on T. V. with Jim Purcell at Newark, N. J.

Feb. 22, 1951

Breakfast in Pine Room, Hotel Belmont Plaza. 11 a.m. at Blood Bank. 12:30 on T.V. I call on Grace Hudowalski at her Exhibit. I made a record for Italy (Vocal record). 6 p.m. Made five minute Record for Rod and Gun Club.

Feb. 23, 1951

Long Island Exhibitor bring me four oysters. Got cheque for $800.00 from Campbell-Fairbanks. With two men dismantle and pack in 3 hours.

Mar.2, 1951

At Saranac Lake. I make reservation for lower berth on tonight's sleeper to N.Y.C. 9:53 on sleeper. Happy Jolly colored porter is Black—a measure-full of grace.

Mar. 4, 1951

7 p.m. At Versaille Night Club and T.V. (NBZ—WNBT)

Mar. 13, 1951

Saranac Lake: Beauty Walk on Bloomingdale Avenue to opposite Baker mountain. I go over 400 verses of my Poems. I read, write and plan for on-coming season. I paint my Fisherman Hat green.

April 19, 1951

At Saranac Lake: Mid-day—I hear Gen. Douglas MacArthur speak from the Nation's Capitol. The Speech, 42 minutes, was by a man with 52 years military experience—a 5 star General just recently fired by Harry S. Truman, President of the U.S.A. and an American Ass. The Speech was most appropriate and by far the best ever made by an unreproachable Military General.

May 3, 1951

Malone: Noon—I have dinner with Rotary Club and Vaudville Entertainers. I speak a brief 5 minutes at Franklin Hotel then set up Replica Exhibit. Next day 8-12 at Show I addressed audience twice—"A Bear Eat Me Up" and "Micke swallowed the Blarney Stone." I autograph and sell photos.

May 12, 1951

On train and in N.Y.C. I call N.B.C. 2 p.m. On television at 30 Rockefeller Plaza.

June 27, 1951

At Wilmington. An American smart Liberty Dog in Car near Sidewalk, almost jump in my face as I pass. To Hell with American Liberty!

Sept. 4, 1951

2 p.m. Launch out with Lee Chadeayne for Adirondack Loj. Walk to Indian Falls by Dusk. Supper, campfire, to bed—dream of bears.

Sept 5, 1951

At Indian Falls: Perfect sunshine and Algonquin view. I check 34 kinds of trees, shrubs and grasses within 50 feet of Lean-to. 3 o'clock—Beauty Sleep on ledge near Flume. Sundown I find one gallon jug near Marcy Trail. Two acres of sunshine linger 19 seconds on Algonquin.

Oct. 11, 1951

At Wilmington. Beard trim Cold River style. 7 o'clock. To Keene Valley with Dittmars for ADK gathering at Air Port. Mr. Burt lead Song Feast and at 8 I speak 50 minutes to over 100 people. Refreshments and home to Wilmington.

Nov. 9, 1951

Two American Fools scream on the road; next they enter an old vacant house, then they thumb for a ride. They show in general they are Americans—tough, weak-minded and as foolish as Fool Liberty can produce anywhere.

Dec. 25, 1951

Wilmington: Kids call and get Xmas trees. I play violin. Pecks bring me a big supper.

Jan. 1, 1952

Hear ye, Hear ye—Very mild, breezy, thawing. Snow about gone; brooks roaring at Wilmington, N. Y. I pick up knocked down Replica of Cold River Town Hall and store under cover. Village children call.

Jan. 7, 1952

The day continues full of sunshine at Wilmington. I spend p.m. at Robert Wood and help sew 60 buckskin bags. Mrs. Blanch Peck send me a basin of Baked Beans. A dead Bob Cat hang at Sport and Gift Shop.

Jan. 21, 1952

Last night: Thaw caught cold. I wash garments. 5 village Kids call.

Jan. 28, 1952

Peru man call selling apples. I read "Grit"—it isn't Hell. (N.B. following news headline clipped and pasted on page: "Invisible Government Seen in Busy Washington" Noah's comment: Must be a Visionary Democrat seeing the "Invisible.")

Feb. 7, 1952

A nice Winter Day at Saranac Lake. I call at Grey's, Drutz Groceries, Newberry's, Saranac Supply. I lodge at 4 Alpine Terrace. I receive 50 pieces of mail.

Feb. 20, 1952

Mild and feeble sun through haze at Wilmington. I receive telegram from N.Y.C. Plaza 5-2000 Extension 7123, Mary Rose, Asst. Producer T.V. I wrote Hotel Belmont Plaza N.Y.C.

Feb. 24, 1952

Saranac Lake—New York City. On Trail Way Bus 10 hours and 50 minutes. Many at Hotel remember me of old.

Feb. 25, 1952

Up at 7 o'clock. 8 a.m. Breakfast in Pine Room. 9 a.m. at 1947 Broadway C.B.S. Studio 60. In p.m. see a lot of New York's busy district. Shop on Lexington Avenue. First wearing new Loafer socks.

Feb. 26, 1952

Up at 7 a.m. One bath. Breakfast 9 a.m. off with taxi. 10-12 at 1947 Broadway. 11:30-12 on T.V. 1 p.m. Confab with Mrs. Ella Gross. Get three phone calls. I buy Stetson Hat and Red Glass Bowls.

Feb. 27, 1952

At Belmont Plaza Hotel, N.Y.C. and Troy, where I stop with my Friends the Millers. Happy Evening; Doberts and Denakers call.

April 8, 1952

At Wilmington - Saranac Lake. Nail can, wire-sew a Cold River Can and articulate a wire bail. Put away winter Gloves and Scarf. Evening: Greyhound to Saranac Lake.

April 11, 1952

At Wilmington, N. Y. I have Civilization's Distemper —picked up at Saranac Lake. One year ago Today Gen.

MacArthur was fired by Obnoxious Ass Truman. It's the worst insult the American People ever got from an American weak minded Democratic Ass.

April 22, 1952

Nice Vernal Sun and Breezy at Wilmington. I call at Store. Gary and Bonnie Terry play at my Wigwam. An enthusiastic Lady call for Balsam Pillow. Bonnie make batch of Mud Pies (Sand, Top Soil, Water, Green Grass for Garnishing and Red Birch for Confection Sugar.) Best of all is the little cook. I do Hermit Wash with Broadway Fab.

May 20, 1952

At Hill Top Farm, Ausable Forks, N. Y. I transplant 2 Lilacs, 4 High Bush Craneberry Trees. I help Priscilla (his sister) build a Chick Coop. I prepare home brooders for 236 Chicks. Pear and Pin Cherry Trees and Columbines are in bloom at standard best.

June 2, 1952

With Kerosene Torch I wreck the homes of thousands of Caterpillars. First Baby Robin at large. This day has been somber and cool plus moisture.

June 17, 1952

I put insulation on Cold River Town Hall Replica and I put 75 Chickens there.

June 27, 1952

At Hill Top Ranch. I make concrete foundation for Poultry Ranch. I butcher a Pig. I transplant cabbage. Sundown: Midgets are hot footed.

July 3, 1952

Hill Top Ranch. I do a lot of hard work: Mowing Hay, weeding garden, building Poultry Ranch—Feeding 200 chicks, 2 Pigs, one calf. Feed is high priced and there is so much work attached that success is impossible—very much due to the thief, robber and murderous American goat. St. Patrick (Halsey Payro) bring Ice Cream and Butter Milk. Sumac is a show of light colored perpendicular spikes.

July 11, 1952

At Hill Top. American Hawk got one of my Prize White Leghorns. Give Potato Bugs drink of Paris Green. Set Wigwam Frame in Chick Yard. Evening I go to Cadyville with Payro Family and Sister Priscilla. The Trip was spoiled by 3 fool kids raising Hell in the back seat.

Aug. 12, 1952

At Hill Top Ranch. I advertise—"Chicken for Sale." White Leghorn Pullets 3 months old are just becoming fine singers. Mrs. Collins chase her yearling heifer over Mastoid Ledge. I do chores, walk around and estimate value of my Pig Weeds.

Sept. 7, 1952

Perfect sunshine, perfect Summer Day with Coolness in Air, hardly detectable. Advanced guard of Autumn disguised as Spy in Late Summer Day at Hill Top Ranch. The Hills and Vallies are so wonderful that I hate the foreign name America applied to them.

Sept. 10, 1952

Reading Einstein Second Time. At Hill Top Ranch. —Relativity, Radio-activity, Mass, Energy, Motion, Time, Uranium, Electro-magnetic Field, Galaxies, Interstellar Space—Universe.

2 p.m. Mrs. Lincoln Collins, madder than Moses was when he broke the Slab of Stone that God had just written the Law on, and She Froths Herself into a Mental Monstrosity because I fray her Cow out of My Hay Field.

Sept. 28, 1952

Perfect Autumn Day at Hill Top Ranch. The Hills are putting on red and yellow Skirt Ruffles and waving curt arms in Polly Colors to greet a special Moon. The clock is set back one hour. How much am I offered for all the day light I saved.

Oct. 21, 1952

Cold morning. Ground partly white and sunshine on Colorful Scenes at Hill Top Ranch. I harvest a bag of cattle beets, beet tops and a pail of potatoes. 90% Sumac Leaves are shed. Climax of autumn is passed.

Nov. 2, 1952

Perfect Autumn Day. Cool night. Pumpkins, Dried Corn, Hens molting. Deciduous Trees 83% nude.

Dec. 20, 1952

At Hill Top. Perfect Sunshine, clear and calm. Priscilla McCasland go to Plattsburg to see Mr. Santa Claus. I cut up a Pig's Head. I put hair remover on calf skin. I fry out Pig Fat. I selvage a can of Booth (Boot) Grease. Lord God! How the money rolls in.

Dec. 25, 1952

Hill Top Ranch 2 a.m. 3 O'Neills arrive from Bellmore. 6 a.m. Payros, 3 McCaslands call. 7 p.m. Rick Rack, Miriam, Butch and Peggy — Blow Horns then Christmas Tree's Humming.

Dec. 30, 1952

I look over old mail — Burn old papers. I overhaul boxes in shed. Thaw out cans. 1952 — Twont be long now!

Feb. 11, 1953

Arthur Bensen call and talk Frontier Town business for next season. At Hill Top I watch the wind gather snow in its arms and whirl it in a spiral 20 feet high and then scatter it like vanishing smoke.

Feb. 20, 1953

I call on Dr. Dittmar and he put Plastic Dentures in my mouth; then he make me bite on them and say Mississippi. I'm pretty mad about it.

Feb. 25, 1953

Mid Day at Hill Top. I take 3 hours Beauty Sleep. The sleep worked but the Beauty was a failure.

April 13, 1952

At Hill Top Farm. In Snow storm against gloomy sky, 4 robins pose in an Oak with breasts rounded out like ripening apples.

Aug. 31, 1953

Thanks August for 31 days—Growing corn and Squeaking crickets, Ripening Field and Happy Summer Days.

Dec. 28, 1953

At Lewis, N. Y. Jack and Mrs. Goff and two boys call. We kill so many big deer and bear in living room that I have to walk on livers. Confab late.

Jan. 2-3, 1954

Cloudy, Snowing all day—10 flakes per hour per acre at Lewis, N. Y. I mend blue denim overall. Happy Day. 72 hours snowing=2 inches snow.

Cloudy all day, snowing=1½″. Old Fashion Rabbit Hunt: 4 cars+9 men+6 dogs+9 Guns=4 Rabbit.

Feb. 1, 1954

Ausable Forks. 10 below to 10 above—sunshine on beautiful winter Mountain. I read History.

Feb. 5, 1954

30 above, very cloudy—slight breeze. I add 22 historical quotations to my growing file.

Feb. 17, 1954

Snowed 15″ last night. Pine branches droop with their loads of snow. Today: 7″ more snow. School close.

Mar. 6, 1954

20 to 30 above zero. Clouds—wind—bits of sun. P.M. Snow and wind make blusters as starting to jump over the Moon.

In weeks Robins will come from South; and fray the Snow out of the bluster; And demand sunshine in which to sing and whisper.

11 p.m. Adlai Stevenson speaks in Florida—just like a Democrat—Damn good Liar.

Mar. 7-23, 1954

20 above zero—Sun morning, then very cloudy all day. Mid afternoon: Snow Squall caught the wind—or—wind caught the Snow—the two raise a hell bluster over the Hills.

40 above — very cloudy, long distance visibility — 30 miles.

Mr. John Wingate was at my camp at Cold River Feb. 12, 1947 and I made Vocal Records for Him at my Cold River Town Hall.

April 5, 1954

Au Sable Forks. 42 degrees above zero. Nice sunshine on the Hill. I make batch of Eternity Tea.

April 10, 1954

54 degrees above zero. Very cloudy at Ausable Forks. First Blue Bird on Clothes Line Post. I get large Bear Skin, and Beaver Mittens from my store.

May 24, 1954

Clouds and Sun — Ausable Valley. I set 4 bottom Logs starting Pine Log Cabin. There's a Nest of Baby Robins in the Front Porch.

May 25, 1954

Breezy—A Handful of Sunshine—a Bushel of Clouds in Ausable Valley. I fit second row of Logs on New Cabin.

June 1. 1954

Nice day, rainy evening—Ausable Valley. I overhaul some of my riches. Welcome June Day—stay to July—have a good time. Don't mind the Black Flies.

June 7, 1954

Robins that left nest 5 days ago are good flyers. I overhaul cases and boxes getting ready to move to Wilmington, Adirondack Sportsmen's Show.

June 12, 1954

Ausable Forks—I cut Doorway in Log Cabin.

June 13-16, 1954

I finish Log Cabin ready to move. I carry more Hermit Property to my strong boxes.

I cut stove pipe hole in Cabin roof.

Nice June Day. I do a lot of work getting ready to go to Wilmington. The new hay is good. Birds are singing. Late Spring is beautiful. Summer is coming.

June 17, 1954

Ausable Forks to Wilmington—I take two loads of Hermit Property to Wilmington. Michael Covert, Melvin Peck and Chester Lawrence work for me. We set up 2 cabins.

June 21-26, 1954

A Hot June Day. Wilmington to Saranac Lake. I Greyhound to Saranac, confab: Ed Worthington, Anna Rice, Bill Mullen, Mrs. Jarvis, M. Mannis. Supper at 4 Alpine Terrace. Evening with W. E. Petty — Lake Clear. Rest in "Love Nest."

A.M. hot sun. p.m. Breezy, cloudy, thunder and rain. Lake Clear to Wilmington. Ride to Saranac with W. E. Petty. Confab Frank Blanchard. Hitch Hike to Lake Placid. Dinner at George Williams. Hitch to Wilmington. I miss my Remington 22 Pump Rifle.

At my Wigwam all day. I write 5 letters. I investigate Remington Pump went via back of Town Hall.

Rain last night. Today: Perfect June Sunshine. I prepare poles to hang Exhibit Items.

July 1, 1954

Sunshine and scattered clouds — a nice July day after June.

What's called "Welfare" in Essex County is Miserable Existence. To Hell with it.

July 5, 1954

At Wilmington Sportsmen's Show. 4 times I put out my display and 4 times I pull it in, under cover to escape the rain.

I address a Canadian Audience in French.

Sept. 6, 1954

Perfect sunshine at Wilmington Sportsmen's Show. Two State Troopers drag through. One talk foolish to a bitch near my exhibit.

Adirondack Sportsmen's Show close at 7:00 p.m.

Sept. 21, 1954

Perfect Sunshine at Wilmington, N. Y.

(The following entry is headed "Peter Henderson—9-11-54): Too Dee Mayorrr Mexican Jumping Beans (100) received ok. Now in the hot house. Regards.

Pete.

(This is evidently a note Noah received from Peter Henderson II, postmarked Ray Brook, N. Y.)

Oct. 7, 1954

Last Night: Ist Ice. Today Sunshine, Cold Breeze. Snow on Whiteface. I write Birmingham.

Oct. 28, 1954

Last Night: First Snow on Roofs and at borders—just a Sample. I pack cases to go to Birmingham, Alabama.

Nov. 6-7, 1954

Snow on mountains. I get letter from Birmingham.

I overhaul my voyage equipment to follow the Robins.

Nov. 13, 1954

Perfect day of Sunshine. On Greyhound. Arrive at 42nd st. N.Y.C. 5:45 a.m. I buy ticket and check baggage to Birmingham, Ala. Leave N.Y. 7 a.m.; Ride south New Jersey—flat country. Glimpse Capitol at 2 p..m Night: through Carolinas. I sleep on.

8:30 a.m. stop 2 hours at Atlanta, Ga. Send telegram to L. H. Gillies in Birmingham, Ala. Arrive 2:45. L. H. Gillies, his son and granddaughter meet me at bus station.

Nov. 15, 1954

Splendid rest after 48 hours on Grey Hound Bus. 7 o'clock: Blue Jay call. P.M. I Beauty Sleep. Mr. Leo Willett call for news from the Hermit.

First ever persimmon.

Dec. 14, 1954

At Birmingham, Ala. I shop on 1st avenue. I write Christmas Cards. Mrs. L. H. Gillies looks so young, she could pass for an Old Maid.

Dec. 25, 1954

Temperature 51 degrees, At Birmingham. I walk around 2 blocks. Merry Xmas. The most quiet, serene ever Christmas! Alone with Mr. and Mrs. L. H. Gillies. The most satisfactory Christmas.

Dec. 31, 1954

Birmingham, Ala. The year 1954 was good for me. Many good experiences so that the last half was more satisfactory than the first.

Mar. 6, 1955

(The following was written at Birmingham while visiting L. H. Gillies family. In answer to a news headline "It is a crime to attempt suicide in U.S.A.") : Anyone attempting suicide should make it a success; then U. S. Big Business can't do anything about it; but, in case of failure it's occasion for arrest before Judge, answer questions, listen to rant, pose for photo, contorted writer, fool newspaper, pay fine, go to jail, get lice, bed bugs and coffee not fit to drink. To hell with a country not fit to live in where suicide is not allowed.

Sept. 13, 1955

At Wilmington. (comments after reading headline "Baptists to Hold Christian Hour")—If God ever find that out, He'll be a surprised snooper.

Feb. 17, 1956

At Warren Terry's, Wilmington: Two News Writers from Syracuse and Saranac Lake call on me. Syracuse man take flash photos at my Town Hall Replica.

Mar. 1., 1956

10 p.m. Pres. Eisenhower appear on T.V. and speaks 30 minutes. Speech was beautiful, honest, clear. No Fool show off, no high kick—just Honest Ike.

Mar. 9, 1956

A Bushel of Clouds and a Pinch of Sunshine. I do fancy wash and give myself Haircut Cold River Style. I run foot race with Virginia Peck and Bonnie Terry. I got beat each time.

May 15, 1956

Song Sparrows sing and jingle small change. Spring is 3 weeks late and Fourth of July will be Aug. 15th. I watch weather go by as I pick Frog Feathers.

Sept. 23, 1956

I call at my Town Hall with Gary Terry. Find: Violin smashed, small boxes left open and about 50 holes punched in canvas roof.

Oct. 13, 1956

Wilmington-Keene Valley. To Keene in Terry's car. I call at Library and ride to Garden with Mrs. Jones. Walk to salt lick and mountain views. Lunch at lean-to, supper at Central School. Greenleaf Chase slides, and

Noah J. Rondeau concentrating on Seward Pond trout — 1940.

Rondeau's raft at Seward Pond.

Last minute piscatorial preparations.

Hermit Rondeau and friend E. A. Harmes of Binghamton.

Dr. Orra Phelps in Ouluska Pass, Aug. 30, 1938.

Noah at Big Dam, Cold River, in 1947.

Making little ones out of big ones. June, 1946. E. A. Harmes photo.

Mary Dittmar getting a facial treatment Cold River style, Sept. 5, 1943.

"I guess that will do the job."

Noah's Aunt "Maggie," Mrs. Henry Miner, Au Sable Forks, N. Y., 1867-1963.

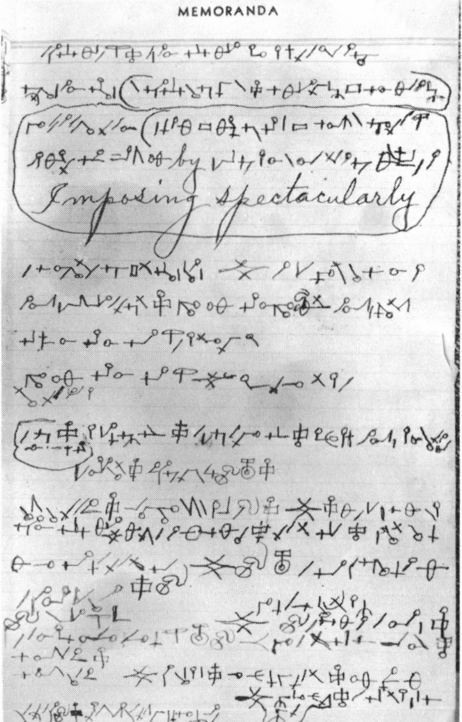

A sample of Noah John's special code called by one friend "the claw marks of an inebriated hen."

A souvenir from Jacques Suzanne of sled dog fame.

The start of Air Lift to fame at New York City Sportsmen's Show at Grand Central Palace, N.Y.C., Feb. 15-22, 1947.

The Hermit and Arlene Whelan at Paramount Studios, February, 1947.

Left to right, Noah and friends at Tahawus Sportsmen's Show: Madeline Dodge, Mary Dittmar, Ditt Dittmar and son David.

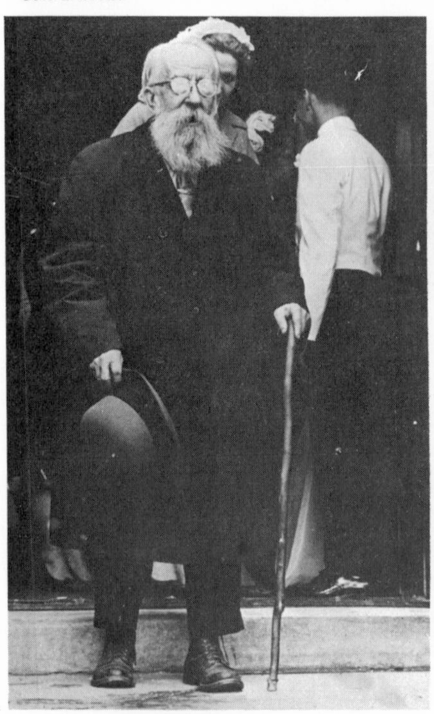

Noah John at Trummer-McCalvin wedding in St. Bernard's Church, Saranac Lake. McLaughlin photo.

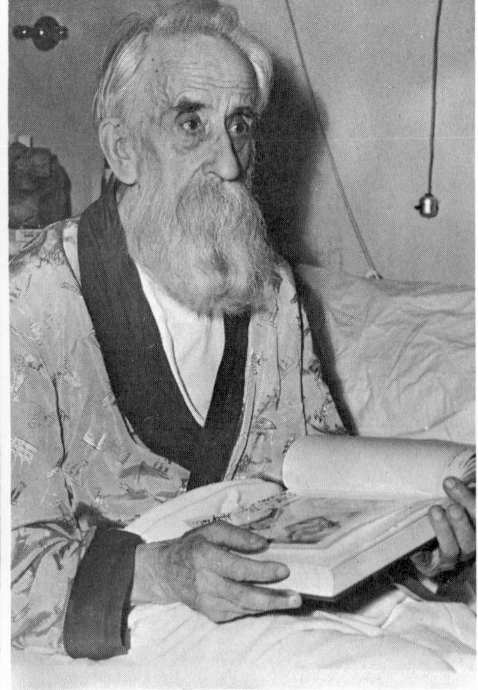

N. J. R. at Lake Placid Memorial Hospital in Aug., 1967, just prior to his death. Photo by Albany TIMES-UNION.

dance. Next day at Ausable Lake take Beauty Sleep on Maple leaves near outlet. Saw big trout in pool below dam on way to Rainbow Falls. Wonderful day with good company of ADK's.

Jan. 6, 1957

20 below. Spills of sunshine and spreads of clouds at Wilmington. Rough Winter Weather.

Jan. 15, 1957

Last night 38 below zero at Wilmington, N. Y. I read and write. Hair cut—beard trim Cold River Styles. Colder than Hell. I rest and lazy about.

Feb. 2, 1957

I get letter from Cantwell lawyers. This is Ground Hog Day and the Woodchuck don't know it.

Feb. 7, 1957

Calm, mild overcast at New York City. 2 a.m. had chowder in Utica. 8 a.m. arrive at Grand Central. 9 a.m. Met Rudy Wiezel at 2 Tudor City Place. 3 o'clock: View several Ocean Liners. 7 o'clock: Dinner at Terrace Restaurant with Wiezel's, then read Poems to 10 p.m.

Feb. 9, 1957

New York City—Milford, N. J. 10 a.m. I sit in car near orchard 40 miles from Tudor City Place. Noon Crunch at Log Cabin Restaurant. Chicadee, Junco, Nuthatch and sparrows all feed near window. 3 o'clock with Rudy and his good Alice we drive to Milford. We lodge at Frederic Dolsen. Chicken dinner, Greek wine. Gab feast to midnight and 30 minutes more for good measure.

Feb. 12, 1957

New York City—Syracuse. I left Tudor City at 10 a.m. Ride with Wiezel to Syracuse. On Thruway sign: Deer Crossing. Bear Mountain, Cat Skill; Dinner with Mrs. Wiezel, Sr. and her son. At Syracuse confab about Sportsmen Show.

Feb. 16, 1957

Wilmington—Saranac Lake. Ride to Saranac Lake with Mrs. Terry and 3 Pecks. Confab with F. B. Cantwell. "No Float, Hard Luck. No cooperation."

Mar. 29, 1957

At Wilmington. I eat and sleep and dream and watch the snow fall. Spring Time and winter weather.

Apr. 17, 1957

At Wilmington, N, Y. Three swarms of Honey Bees come out. Poplars have buds like fuzzy kittens. A Robin first insinuate "Cheer up" song. Grand Mom Lewis' Gran Daughter come see me 1st time and I buy her for 5c.

May 31, 1957

At Wilmington. Temperature is perfect and vernal green perfect too. Ten year old Boy going up the walk with a Fish Pole on his shoulder and a chippin' sparrow hop on the cement 10 feet ahead of me. Little black flies are here and how they love us.

Aug. 10, 1957

Hot summer day at Wilmington. I water flowers, feed Honey Bees, watch the Birds and listen to the Crickets. (Very much like summer).

Sept. 1, 1957

Perfect sunshine at Grafton. Big Clam Steam. 27 People—song Feast and beer. Dance, jump and hop to midnight. Good crowd, good spirit, good time.

Sept. 14, 1957

At Wilmington. I feed Honey Bees and watch Adirondack Hills putting on color to greet Autumn. 7 p.m. a TV Picture of the Adirondacks and explained by Dick Young is good.

Oct. 4, 1957

At Wilmington. Today Russians gave first kick to first ball that went out of Atmosphere as a young moon.

Oct. 5, 1957

Keene Valley. Register at Library. Ride to Ausable Lake. Cross Outlet for Random Scoot. 6:30 at Central School. Big dinner—over 400 people put a lot of food in their faces and out of sight.

Oct. 13, 1957

At Wilmington. I watch for Sputnik 8:40 to 9:05 S.T. At 9:05 I saw a glimpse that may be Sputnik—chances are it was Plane or Baloon in sunshine a long way off and only a glimpse. Time reveals I saw Sputnik but just a brief glimpse.

Nov. 24, 1957

At Wilmington. Morning rain, mid day squall blanch fields and roofs. Rough weather late in Autumn. A bit of sun, busy breeze, snow like smoke brushing over roofs. Somber clouds wrap up Mountain Tops.

Dec. 22, 1957

Wilmington. I call at Lake Placid Memorial Hospital—see Choppy Preston and Gary Terry. Beautiful is Panorama of Mountains as seen from Hospital and Lake Placid to Wilmington.

Dec. 25, 1957

At Wilmington. Joe Williams call on me to confab about George Morgan. I had a very good Christmas season.

Dec. 28, 1957

At Wilmington. I trim my new Diary with clippings from 2 Almanacs. Black dog (Friskie) is sick.

Jan. 21, 1958

Wilmington, N. Y. Packing to change Terry's. I pack several boxes of Hermit Riches and burn rubbish. I quit boarding at Carl Terry's. I take down my two paintings from his living room.

Feb. 12, 1958

At Wilmington. I red silk date in new underwear. I make a medical food Chowder.

Mar. 4, 1958

City of Wilmington. I read, write, eat, sleep and inspect fishing tackle.

Mar. 22, 1958

At Wilmington. I inspected Peck's little barn and find bloody wings of last of 5 doves killed and eaten by domestic American Cat.

Apr. 17, 1958

At Wilmington. Man from Enchanted Kingdom call to get me for summer. Bonnie Terry beat me in our first foot race of season.

May 19, 1958

At Wilmington. I ride to Lake Placid. Confab Skip O'Hare, Beautiful ride back: Wilmington Notch,—Mountains—Vallies—Vernal Green—Shad Blossoms.

May 23, 1958

At Black Brook. At William Rondeau's several people call. Confab Chester, Burton Orville, Mrs. Savage. We spin big Yarns.

June 3, 1958

At Wilmington. A variety of birds confab in several languages in Elm Trees. Aging dandelions put on fuzzy white heads. Two Mosquitoes call in my room. I put 16 redheads on 16 Bouquets of Feathers on 16 Trolling Rigs.

July 8, 1958

Wilmington. I get belated Birthday Cake and writing paper.

Aug. 13, 1958

At Wilmington. I listen to President Eisenhower's speech to U. N. It was a Master Speech.

Sept. 26, 1958

Wilmington. I undress two chickens. Morgan mountain trimmed with Maple Red and Ever Green.

Oct. 5, 1958

At Wilmington. Mid Day: First fine snow in the Air. I patch green checkered shirt. I go to old wool underwear.

Nov. 15, 1958

At Wilmington. I do a lot of sleeping while the weather goes by.

Nov. 27, 1958

Wilmington. We devour an 18 13/16 pound Turkey at Warren Terry's. This Autumn weather feel like Winter.

Dec. 24, 1958

Wilmington. We have Christmas Tree. Pictures, gifts, young and old are very busy. Five year old Melvin Peck is busiest of all.

Jan. 26, 1959

30 degrees below last night. Very cold at Wilmington, N. Y. Windows have frost pictures garnished with frost feathers.

Jan. 31, 1959

Mr. Enoch Squires call on me most of afternoon. We make three tape records. Big visit about Hermit Life, Adirondack Mountains, Vallies, Flora, Fauna. Fishing, Hunting, Trapping and Wig Wams and Cabins; And Astronomy overhead (Cold River Style).

Feb. 3, 1959

Nice Sunshine—cold air—breezy evening at Wilmington. I get 6 loads of my riches from Francis Peck's rooms.

Feb. 19, 1959

10 below last night. Nice sunshine today. I'm packing a few of my riches to go to Westport.

April 14, 1959

High 56 degrees. Slightly breezy—nice sunshine at Wilmington. I doff wool underwear. I don longhandle cotton.

June 1, 1959

4 p.m. Mr. Lee Brow call on me and he presents me with a cane and membership card to "Cane Club."

June 21, 1959

Semi-overcast haze and distant clouds. Very warm. I destroy and banish a box full of old papers.

June 25, 1959

I use a bushel of Snow Ice around Sun Flower Plants to water plants as Snow melt; Snow came conveniently for defrosting Frigidaire.

I'm sorting out Cold River Relics.

July 2, 1959

Long Lake, N. Y. I go to Blue Mt. Lake with Roy Lash. We call at Adirondack Museum. Confab with Mr. Bruce Inverarity for 90 minutes; And I left 60 items with director of Museum. We visit museum for 90 minutes.

Aug. 2, 1959

At Wilmington. John Blackburn call on me; and he introduce over a dozen People from China, Germany, Austria, Holland and Jordan. And a doctor from Egypt.

Oct. 22, 1959

A nice Autumn day. Ice on 2/3 of Wilmington Lake. Morgan Mountain has lost all its crimson. I go to wool underware.

Nov. 2, 1959

1 p.m. Granules of snow bigger than cabbage seeds dance on outside window. I sew Fancy Fronts on my Alabama Sweater-Coat.

Nov. 11, 1959

Wilmington. Sunshine, nice autumn weather. I eat and sleep. It's too tiresome to work between meals.

Dec. 25, 1959

Wilmington. Mrs. Terry Roasts a Turkey. Santa don't bring me nothing—not even an old Maid.

Jan. 20, 1960

At Wilmington. I write "How to Build Wigwam" to my Friend Vincent Steers, Spenard, Alaska. I make Hermit Soup. I quilt 2 shirts together.

April 14, 1960

At Wilmington. A Big Boy stoled Marbles from Chipper Peck and he got away. Chipper chased the thief but he got away. Mrs. Peck had to chase to bring 7 year old Chipper back home.

June 1, 1960

At Wilmington. Young and old Starlings raise hell within house walls.

July 17, 1960

At Wilmington: Three men from Cadyville call on way Trout Fishing. Chipper Peck call for Fish Line and Fish Hooks. Later he call for 10 cents.

Nov. 24, 1960

Wilmington. I helped Mrs. Pelkey finish moving my riches. Mrs. Pelky cook a Thanksgiving Dinner that was not hard to take.

Nov. 29, 1960

To Saranac Lake. Confab Frank Blanchard and lunch with him. Confab Helen McCalvin, Bill Mullen. Good visit with Capt. Lampford, who go tomorrow to trap line (Cold Brook—Sawtooth Mountain).

Dec. 24, 1960

Wilmington. I stay indoors alone all day. I doll up a bit. 7-9 p.m. We have Christmas Tree at Jennie Pelkey. Her son and 4 daughters and in-laws and Grandchildren all come to see Santa. All receive gifts and we have bit of modest liquor.

Dec. 31, 1960

Wilmington, N. Y., I clean half my Bed Room floor and move and settle some of my riches. Quietude is serene. Good Night 1960.

Jan. 31, 1961

Wilmington, R. G. Wiezel called on me and we confab about Alexander Rondeau working at Kilns and producing Charcoal which was used by J. & J. Rogers Co. to semi-process crushed iron into pig iron about 90 years ago. And we chatted about Peter Rondeau's barrel of cisco for the Holy Season of Lent of 1893.

April 2, 1961

I go to Nazarene church and listen to children speaking and singing Easter subjects. Little tots in Easter Bonnets and Butterfly skirts were Sweet Little Speakers.

I go back to Old Wool after 12 days in long handle cotton.

April 10, 1961

Mrs. Wayne H. Byrne from Plattsburgh call on me and for 3 hours we plan on writing "Cold River Hermit."

May 2, 1961

Saranac Lake. Call at Presbyterian Church with Janitor Colby. See where Calvin Coolidge worshipped in 1926.

May 14, 1961

Pine Ridge Cemetery, Saranac Lake. I confab Paul Dupree and buy Grave Plot to bury an old carcass.[1]

June 15, 1961

Bill Petty sit in my new rocking chair and he tells me a big bear story about a Big Bear. He also bring me a typewriter—Remington Portable to use as I please. Thank you, Mr. Petty. I wash 9 pieces Fabric.

---

[1] According to Mr. Dupree, Noah never did buy a plot. He was buried in North Elba Cemetery.

Aug. 20, 1961

6:30 Supper at Hawkeye Lodge: 7:30 93 girls, 2 young men and Director (over 100) congrate (i.e. congregate) on Docks and in 7 canoes. A Torch is lighted on a little flat and the Girls sing Campsongs. Mountains are hazy, weather threatening rain. First shade of night is spread. The Hermit is introduced and speaks 45 minutes as shades of night close in. And we go to large living room, fireplace and cheerfulness. I write autographs, drink more coffee.

Nov. 5, 1961

Wilmington. For first time I wear Fool American License on my back and take my gun for a short hunt in woods at Sundown. At night I do much sewing on Red Hunting Jacket.

Jan. 17, 1962

At Haselton: I eat and sleep and write and laugh at theories about mythical Gods. I made a bowl of Eternity Tea.

Jan. 24, 1962

I go to Saranac Lake. Confab Mrs. H. Moody and call on Charles Green and have Old Time confab. Kelly Bowen comb my hair and wiskers.

April 21, 1962

At Haselton. Water Frogs Hoarsely grind their teeth in Willow Marsh. Warren Terry bring home a Puppy. Puppy trap self under a chair.

May 30, 1962

At Buck Hill. Tom Conway call. Had not seen him in over 57 years. And in short hour we thrashed a lot of news and revived memories of 60 years ago.

July 4, 1962

At Cadyville: I take pin curlers off my Whiskers. I comb my Whiskers in style. Hurrah! Fourth of July.

July 8, 1962

At Haselton: At Markenville Cemetery for Funeral of Adrian Lawrence. Large funeral, big crowds, many cars, a load of Flowers. Every one Well Dressed and all orderly and beautiful—plus well controled. Deep Sorrow of Relatives and Friends; and the general sadness that accompany Death and Burial.

July 29, 1962

Harold Fortune call me on telephone and wants me to take roll of Santa Klaus at North Pole. My answer: I am sorry, Mr. Fortune but I am not accepting any work. The reason: I worked 65 days last year at White Face Museum and the visitors, the sponsor and the pay was all satisfactory until the so-called Welfare Authority of Essex County made it so unsatisfactory that I cannot work under the circumstances. I have been poorer for months, and I'm poorer now than I would be if I did not work in 1961.

Aug. 23, 1962

At Haselton. I am quite sick with Stomach and Bowel disorder.

Aug. 27, 1962

Ausable Forks—Plattsburgh. Dr. Dittmar call for me and take me to Plattsburgh. 12:30 we dine with Rotary Club at Cumberland Hotel. 1:30 I speak "40 years" in 35 minutes. Good crowd—perfect audience. 2:30 Dr. Dittmar extract my last 8 teeth.

Oct. 9, 1962

Mr. Clifford E. Smith and myself stay up to nearly midnight killing Big Bucks. By 11 p.m. living room linoleum was nearly all covered with deer liver. Next evening we look at good rifles and we tell big stories about big deer and big bear.

Dec. 13, 1962

At Wilmington. Richard Smith and Lord Burguiere spend afternoon and evening with me and we spin yarns.

Jan. 24, 1963

A tug of war: argument between Priscilla McCasland and Clayton Burnah. Priscilla get stick to thrash C.C. take hold of other end stick. Tug of war last 2 minutes. P. weaken, C. gets stick. Then he won't sit down until she meet his stipulation not to hit him after he sit down. Clayton come back vocally "if you hit me I throw your radio and smash it."

June 19, 1963

River Road, Lake Placid (Abe Fuller's). Today Sunshine, gentle breeze, like modest wind cause leaves to twist and spin on poplar trees like coins hung on strings. I walk about the garden and gloat about my riches. I throw a potato digger at a rabbit and hustle him out of my garden.

July 18, 1963

7 p.m. Abraham Fuller says "Your wood has come." I say, "I did not order wood." Then Abe to Wood Man—"He has changed his mind again," and Abe rants at my expense.

Aug. 11, 1963

At Silver Lake. At early dusk a young lady introduce the speaker (me). She almost got stuck but she done a perfect job. The trouble? She had to present a Rube Specimen with Whiskers as an Orator from the Sticks and that's no easy job. Then I spoke nearly an hour to 75 young ladies all sitting on the floor in front of glowing fire. Loving happiness was felt thanks to Harmony in every one.

Aug. 31, 1963

River Road. Early morn. Abe Fuller glue his fool face to my window and squint to see what he can snoop.

Sept. 6, 1963

Evening. Abraham Fuller cover his cucumber vines; there are no cucumbers on the vines. There has not been any cucumbers on the vines. But he covers the vines. (nice vines, Abe. . .)

Nov. 13, 1963

Singing Pines, Wilmington. I wash 10 pieces Fabric. I cut Wigwam Poles and make Trap Sauce (scent). I pin license to jacket. I chop stove wood. Mr. Denton and son James bring me two pig's heads. Evening I carve and classify cuts of pork.

Dec. 3, 1963

At Singing Pines. I find the winter scene perfect. The 12 foot spruce 10 feet from the cabin door is decked in perfect Xmas style. And the chalk-white birches among Singing Pines in the concave of the semi circle of the Road is perfect scene for the Hermit to view through the Little Cabin's Window. I start sour dough to generate yeast to raise my winter pan cakes.

Feb. 7, 1964

I receive cheque for miserable existence from "Big Business" so called Welfare. I shop in seed catalogs.

Feb. 12, 1964

At Singing Pines. And here it is: Ash Wednesday and no ashes to rub on my fool head and no ciscoes for the Holy Season of Lent. If God find that out He will raise Hell.

May 9, 1964

At Singing Pines. A handful of clouds and a bushel of sunshine. The Forest's vernal green dance to the tunes of May Breeze, while the songs of a multiplicity of birds make hills and vallies ring. Richard Smith (owner of Singing Pines) call and we have laughing visit.

Aug. 11, 1964

At Singing Pines. Mr. and Mrs. Wiezel arrive from Lake Ontario via Heart Lake. We sit among silver birches, relax and take a nip of bourbon. We drive to Keene Valley and dine at Spread Eagle Inn. We drive to Garden (2 miles) and Wiezel hit trail to John's Brook Lodge.

Oct. 18, 1964

Perfect autumn Sunday at Singing Pines. I read 15 chapters of Revelations by St. John. First Bible Reading in 27 years.

Oct. 24, 1964

I keep Sabbath. First time in 27 years.

Apr. 22, 1965

At Singing Pines. Summer time is here. It's good to see a Robin on a green lawn. Snow all gone in the vallies but lots of snow on Whiteface Mountain. Many Spring and Summer birds are here and for a few days more will resurrect the shrubs that were dead and dress them with leaves and put flowers on their heads.

Apr. 28, 1965

At Wilmington. What a wonder! We have news papers to tell us every year when to push our clocks ahead and alternating, when to push them back. Such wisdom! Sun, Moon and Stars are Amazed!

Nov. 2, 1965

Singing Pines. I eat and sleep—it's too tiresome to work between meals. And it's American Fool Election Day.

Nov. 11, 1965

Bear hunter Lewis call for pointers on skinning a bear. He kilt a bear last Saturday. Yes, bring your bear in camp under Singing Pines. We skinned and carved the bear—Cold River Style and bear hunter went home happy.

Jan. 24, 1966

Singing Pines. I broom a foot of snow out of 100 feet of trail around Cabin and to public road. A man from Upper Jay shoot his camera at me. Eaves of camp well garnished with icicles. Chicadee birds call for food.

Mar. 8, 1966

Singing Pines. I read and write and see first chipmonk. Saw his tracks 10 days ago. At midday a rabbit try to run over me in my orchard.

April 19, 1966

Mr. Flavin, from Erie, Pa., taxi me home from Madeline Dodge's and for his pay I let him feed my chickadee birds.

May 11, 1966

Singing Pines. I soak 4 grape vines, 1 pear tree and 6-in-1 apple tree. I plant them. I also plant 3 blueberry plants, 1 red dogwood and 4 purple lilacs. Lady from Essex County Welfare call on me.

June 5, 1966

At 8 a.m. Clifford Smith call for me and I go to his home for the day near Haystack mountain. And what purple lilacs and old time covered bridge through Upper Jay past Noble Denton's—Lilacs and Lilacs and Haystack Mt.

Aug. 15, 1966

Last night my best ripe tomatoes disappeared from plant.

Oct. 9, 1966

Mr. and Mrs. R. G. Wiezel call and we sit among silver birches and singing pines and have a splendid visit.

Nov. 18, 1966

The walk to Wilmington was every step too much for Old Man.

Dec. 19, 1966

4 p.m. A lady from White Face Methodist Church bring me a Xmas package artistically prepared.

Dec. 25, 1966

Today total overcast. Snowed 10 inches last night. Forest decked in Xmas style. The most beautiful Xmas storm ever at Singing Pines. I broom trails about camp and get wood for the night.

* * * * * * * * * *

The missing journal covering the final eight months of Rondeau's life (Jan.-Aug. 1967) undoubtedly contains much material of interest. His remarks to those who interviewed him at the Lake Placid hospital during the final phase indicated that the entries were being made regularly and in considerable length.

It is regrettable that his comments and observations for that period are not available because they would certainly add considerably to our understanding of his character as it responded to the awareness of approaching death.

Besides his visitors several of the nursing staff at the hospital also were deeply impressed by his cheerfulness and optimism. What he selected to record in his diary is now of course mainly a matter of personal speculation.

Surmising that the last diary was probably the most typical and fascinating of them all, this biographer is convinced that the Rondeau reflected in the journals represents the best index we have to an appreciation and appraisal of Rondeau the man.

THE RONDEAU CORRESPONDENCE

Besides maintaining his diary-journals over a considerable span of years, Noah was also a very active letter-writer. Since most of the letters received by him were either discarded at the time of his numerous changes of residence or destroyed by relatives during the clean-up operation following his death, it is impossible to determine the entire scope of his correspondence and correspondents. It is, however, apparent that he wrote and received a formidable number of letters.

Moreover, like the diaries, these letters also provide a valuable index to his varying moods and range from the exuberantly pleasant and witty to the explosively unpleasant and vitriolic. Examples of the former are those he sent to the Hudowalskis and the Dittmars; the latter are represented by the one he sent to J. M. Kelley of Syracuse concerning the Victory Garden suggestion facetiously suggested by Billy Burger.

The series of letters in which Noah periodically blasted the Conservation Department during the 1920's must have been real gems of the art of invective and probably generated many lively moments and lengthy discussions —particularly among the personnel of the Game Protection Division.

Undoubtedly Rondeau unleashed his strongest verbal weapons at the Tupper Lake game protector who accused the Hermit of character assassination. On that occasion, as Noah told Burger years later, Noah John used over 30 pages to state in easily understood terms precisely what he thought of that individual and his reputation. (see p. 74). What a collector's item that diatribe would be! The same remark would also apply just as aptly to the seven-page missive Rondeau reportedly dispatched the same day to the Conservation Department itself.

There is certainly ample proof that Noey not only had a way with words but that he gave them plenty of practice. As the selections indicate he had a remarkable range and fluency of expression which enabled him to adjust readily to each passing and dominant mood. And as such the accompanying letters contribute considerably to our understanding and appreciation of Noah John Rondeau.

January 12th, 1939
Coreys, N. Y.

Dear Mr. Dittmar:

Blow your nose and Brace up quick! And look your Best. The Mayor of Cold River is arriving in His full Leather Dress. He Smells Wig Wam Smoke and His Whiskers are full of Deer Hair.

Well, How Da Do?

I received the Magic Book, and Photographs; clippings & etc.

I thank you Mr. Dittmar.

Last season I killed a Deer and a Bear.

I had a Bang Up Good Big Supersize Christmas at Bartlett Carry Club near the Saranac River.

Will soon go back in Hermitage for another year.

Best Wishes to You Old Timer

Very Truely
N. J. Rondeau

P. S. Don't forget where the Town Hall is in 1939. (Between Big Dam and City Gate.)

Henry G. Rogers
Au Sable Forks, N. Y.

May 23, 1939

Mrs. Grace L. Hudowalski
c/o Adirondack Mountain Club
Room 1935, 120 Broadway
New York, N. Y.

My Dear Mrs. Hudowalski:

In glancing through the Year Book of the Adirondack Mountain Club for 1939 I was interested in your article on the "Hermit of Cold River" and particularly so in the picture of the Hermit.

Since you are interested enough to write an article regarding him, it has occurred to me that it might perhaps be of passing interest to you to know a little more of his history.

To do this, I must go back to the Hermit's grandfather, who, like all the rest of the family from his generation down to the great-great grandchildren, have most of them worked for our Company, many of them all their lives, having never worked for any other employer.

The Hermit's grandfather, Alex Rondeau, was as picturesque and characteristic a French "habitant" as any that Drummond or Van Dyke ever wrote of. I knew him well for many years and until a short time before his death he worked directly under me in our sulphite mill. He knew only a few words of English.

He had seven sons and one daughter. One of the sons, Peter, was a blacksmith and worked for us all his life.

His wife died, leaving him with five boys and three daughters, the youngest being 20 months old when the mother died, leaving the oldest daughter, not more than 12 years old, to keep house for her father and this large family.

Two of the Hermit's brothers have worked all their lives for us and are now holding responsible positions in our sulphite mill.

Since I have gone this far, I might add that one of the brothers, Charley, has just died in Canada, leaving no issue, but reputedly leaving several houses and other possessions and I believe that yesterday one of the brothers started on a search for the Hermit, with the idea that the family would combine and see if they could get possession of what Charley has left.

Trusting this may be of passing interest to you, I am,

Sincerely yours,
Henry G. Rogers

Jan. 8th, 1940
Coreys, N. Y.

Mr. Edward Hudowalski
82-7th Ave.
Troy, N. Y.

Dear Mr. Hudowalski (Old Mt. Climber)

Christmas time I received the P. O. order you sent me; also the neat little folder, with sixteen names and fifteen little Photographs.

I thank You and each Dear One represented in sending me this splendid Gift.

And I will write every one of them a chunk of my mind. I came out from Cold River Dec. 21st. And I had a Splendid Christmas at Bartlett Carry Club.

It is very wintery here now. The ice is twelve inches thick on Saranac Lakes and we have a foot of snow. And the last two weeks, most of the nights have registered below zero.

After you called at the wigwam last August, I made two climbs to the top of Couchsachraga; once with the Clements Bros., and once with Mr. Street and a Mr. Lynch.

I'm going back to my City in two or three weeks.

And now I'm closing with my Best Wishes for You and Mrs. Hudowalski for The New Year—1940.

I am Greatfully Yours
N. J. Rondeau

Feb. 1st, 1940. 10 p.m.

This is N. J. Rondeau Sitting on a Bear Skin in the Town Hall at Cold River, addressing Mrs. Grace L. Hudowalski of 82 Seventh Ave., Troy, N. Y. and saying—
Dear Old Lady of the Wigwam,

Mr. W. H. Burger and Mr. Abbott are here with me. We left Bartlett Carry Club early Yesterday morning. We went three miles by automobile, then seventeen miles on Skis and Snow-Shoes. It was a day of Sun-Shine (Ideal winter day). The Trees and Mountains were in Their winter best.

Three miles before we reached the Town Hall the sun had hidden from our view, and Panther Peak had a glorious cap of rosy pink. We got in one hour after dark.

We soon had a good fire in each Cabin. Put in good night.

Today: Has been a Happy Day at Camp. My Friends are going back to Bartlett Club tomorrow.

I have my 14 letters "To be Opened" and so far as I know I'm set for a long happy winter. Thank you for Your many kind favors. Best regards to You and Brother Edward.

Very Truly
N. J. Rondeau

Good Night!

July 19th, 1940 2 p.m.

Dear Mrs. Hudowalski

This is the Mayor of Cold River; I am on the Peak of Couchsachraga. Mr. Edward A. Harmes and son John of Binghamton are with me. They just became 46ers indeed. They came to my wigwam yesterday.

July 20th

Rain last night, grass and trees dripping wet. Mountain Climbers going out (10 a.m.)

N. J. Rondeau

November 14th, 1941
Cold River Town Hall

Mrs. Grace L. Hudowalski
82 7th Ave.
Troy, N. Y.

Just a few lines in a hurry to send out by Dr. Lattimer: And to say—I thank you!

Early in August I sent my order for supplies, to Mr. Burguiere in New York, And He had hard luck and He's not coming for a hunt this season. So He sent the order to Dr. Latimer. I wanted food for winter and expected to pay for it. But Dr. Latimer wrote 3 or 4 of my Friends and They all sent Him money; and several people that Dr. L. knew nothing about wrote Him, that "They wanted to Come in."

They sent so much that Dr. L. Could not bring all of it in, in food stuff; it would over fill the car. And He had to have room for His own Stuff for a two weeks Hunt. So He brought my winter supplies all paid for and a handful of money.

Please give my thanks to all. I expect to go out in about 5 weeks and Christmas will be drawing near and it's just like some ADK's and Your Good For Nothing 46ers to send as much more for Christmas; please don't let them do it Grace. They have sent too much. They owe me nothing.

They think I do a lot for them And the fact is, all I do or can do, is—Gass Them vocally and smoke Them in The Wigwam.

On Oct. 16th a party of Forest Rangers, Newspaper Men and the State Airplane Pilot stationed at Lake Placid call on me. By this time there may be a write up in a N. Y. Paper; all about "a Handsome Man". If you see it accordingly don't think it's just a Funny Paper with "My Dear Gaston."

On Oct. 20th My Deer Hunting License was dropped from an airplane at The Town Hall.

Dr. Latimer was surprised and pleased at the results He got. He said "You have more Friends than Roosevelt." and I added—"Yes and Hitler along with Him" And—"My Friends are real; They are not whipped in an Army Camp or bought in a CCC camp. They smell smoke a little bit, because they are just made wigwam fashion."

Enough! Now I must make a Cold River envelop. Love to You and Your Edward.

Sincerely yours
N. J. Rondeau

Dec. 28th, 1941
Coreys, N. Y.

Mr. Adolph G. Dittmar Jr.
8522 106th Street
Richmond Hill, L. I. N. Y.

Dear Dr. Dittmar:

The Mayor of The Town Hall came out Dec. 19th. I Got your letter and Christmas Card; Thank You for The Photographs, The Clippins and all the Good Things.

I am now at Lewis (near Elizabethtown). I had a very good Christmas. Had several cards and letters from The Rough Necks and Tough Mugs of Pennsylvania and Vermont. They make threats to invade me again.

About 100 people registered at the wigwam last season; only one in the whole bunch was bold enough to come three times!

Well I got an 8 point buck in November. I also got a racoon.

Last February a N. Y. Radio wrote me to go to N. Y. and speak on the air; I got the letter in October. In November another Station sent a Guide from Corey's to Cold River to get me to Speak; I could not come out then. As it is now, I expect to go in January but don't know the date yet.

Jan. 2nd, 1942

Well, I will try to finish this letter which I started last year.

I am still at Lewis; and have been visiting many of my Old Friends. Dec. 29th I made several calls on Friends at Elizabethtown—in the evening, The Men's Club was having a dinner; So I went with my Friends. The President and others of Elizabethtown had been Fishermen at Cold River; So I had a good start.

I was seated at a Special Table with The Village President, and (if you please) four Ministers. One of The Rev's was to be the main speaker. (I knew nothing about it). I was put up first for a Speech. And I gassed Them for 20 minutes; Cold River fashion.

I will go back to Upper Saranac Lake in a few days. Last Evening, we had our annual reunion at Westport at the Pipemakers. It was a Splendid Supper and Happy Evening.

I may write you a line later if I get something new on my state. For now, Thank you for your letter and Photography.

Very Truly—
N. J. Rondeau

A Happy New Year to You

Jan. 27th, 1942

NOAH JOHN RONDEAU
Mayor of Cold River
Coreys, New York

Mrs. Grace L. Hudowalski
82-7th Ave.
Troy, N. Y.

Dear Mrs. Hudowalski:

After you left Cold River on Oct. 4th, Things went on about as you might imagin. But a few things happened that might bear mention.

On Oct. 16th six men came along,—three Rangers, one State Plane Pilot and two Newspaper Men with Cameras. They took a lot of Pictures and Notes. Four days later the plane glided over The Town Hall and dropped my Deer Hunting License.

In November Dr. Latimer came along with my Groceries, all paid for, and some money besides; And that made a big difference with my cash receipts for the year. Of course there is no money in what I do these times; and can't be expected But last year was very satisfactory. I had good Trout Fishing and the Vegetables and Flowers were good. And I had a lot of nice visitors.

Dec. 19th I came out to Upper Saranac Lake. And on Christmas Day I went to Lewis. I stayed two weeks; and took in Big Dinner and Men's Clubs at Lewis, Elizabethtown and Westport. I had a splendid time. They wanted me to speak to them; so on four occasions I gave them a Stomachfull, mostly about the Mountains and Valleys.

I notice more and more People have Their Ears open to hear about The Mountains and Valleys and the hundreds of subjects that are among Them. They seem to think that I was a Prince from Mars. And They loaded me with things; Including a portable Radio to take to Cold River.

The only drawback I got a Nasty Civilization Distemper; That I never get up to Cold River and always get when I come out. I came back to Upper Saranac Lake Jan. 9th. I'm just getting over my cold.

I still have quite a lot of writing to do and I'm going back to Cold River some time next month.

Now concerning the money you sent Dr. Latimer. I don't know just who is who in every case. I can imagin the whole 46ers Club came in. I will write several of Them; but some may escape my Pen.

Thank You and Your generous Organization and Please give Them my Hearty Thanks accordingly.

Closing—Good Luck to You and Brother Edward.

Sincerely,
N. J. Rondeau

P. S. in November I got an 8 point Buck.

Thursday, March 18, 1943

RECORD-POST, Au Sable Forks, N. Y.

The Adirondacker
Victory Garden at Cold River by Billy Burger

Hon. Noah J. Rondeau
Mayor of Cold River,
City Hall,
Coreys, N. Y.

Dear Noah:—

I see by the papers that the rationing program is causing you concern. Indeed, it may be delaying your return to your fair city. This is giving me anxious moments for several reasons which I shall hereinafter disclose.

The other day I encountered our mutual friend, Frank Gibson, in the Westport office. Because of his numerous responsibilities and consequent voluminous mail he seems to be "in and out" of there a great deal. As you know, he heads the U.S.O., the YMCA, various and sundry athletic leagues, the work of the Social Service Committee, and still has time to preach a good many sermons on Sunday. Quite a man, I say, and I know you agree.

Frank has recently added another to his formidable list of functions,—namely, that of coordinator of the Victory Garden Campaign in Essex County: Frank is a good man for this, for just like some of the rest of us, he hasn't always won his battles with the bugs and weeds. Naturally he's looking for every recruit he can enlist, so he said to me, "Did you see the article about Noah Rondeau in The Record?" "Sure," I said. "How about signing him up for a Victory Garden?" said Frank. "Swell," said I. "I'll write him," chuckled Frank, "and send him a lot of stuff.:" For once I kept my mouth shut, but thought, "I'll write him, too, but put my letter in the paper. It will take up space during a very lean literary period.

I know you grow pansies and other nice flowers. And some vegetables. But now I'm appealing to you to put in a diversified garden, which will not only supply your needs but those of your guests, who now include not only the 46'ers, the A.M.C.'ers, the C.C.C.'ers and the Burgers, but also the Rockefellers—no less! Certainly you can't afford to ignore the nutritional needs of such a distinguished array of Adirondackers. You must realize that they will come to you this summer with very depleted packs. I doubt if any of them will be burdened by the canned spinach, corn, etc. which they generally lug through the woods. When the succulent greens of your Victory Garden greet their jaundiced eyes, the old saliva will run right down their chins, and how they will disgorge their more or less ill gotten cash. They will revel in fresh vegetables and you will revel in hard coin.

There's another and even more important angle of this matter which I must press upon you. It's very possible that the rationing board in Tupper Lake would be susceptible to a little deal. You agree to raise so many vegetables for so many rationing points, 50 per cent in advance, 50 per cent in the fall when you lay in your staples. Of course, they may be so befuddled by their own ration points that they may not see yours. But anyway, it's worth a good trial.

Far be it from me to suggest the vegetables you'd raise, but I submit a list from a Quaker garden in Bucks county, Pennsylvania, in 1685. Sage, camomile, thyme, comfrey, rue, yarrow and love apples. These are mostly out of my line, but Jean and her pals and I would appreciate some pals and I would appreciate some golden bantam corn when we visit you in September. To eat this with Slam Bang Gullion at Cold River.

Thursday, Mar. 18, 1943

THE RECORD-POST, Au Sable Forks, N. Y.

Public Forum

Syracuse, New York
March 14, 1943

Adirondack Record
Ausable Forks, N. Y.

After reading your article in an early March issue about the problem confronting Noah Rondeau, the hermit, and his drastic situation regarding the point rationing system, as by hibernating in Cold River wilderness, could not appear to shop at certain dates. I think I have a very logical answer to the situation. While this plan might not have a special appeal to Mr. Rondeau, I still think it is right and proper as other folks would see it too. Why does Mr. Rondeau have to hibernate at this time, is not this his war we are in as well as millions of others? Why is he exempt from any obligations to the war effort, is it not his freedom we are fighting for? Physically able? Yes. Too old? No, as I happen to know. I am working along side of men ten years his senior that are doing a real job. Surely he can find some menial task to help. Possibly to relieve someone who could do a real job. Too much of a sacrifice? I don't think so. Not more than some others are doing, leaving their home, their business going on the rocks and dozens of other conditions that Americans and others are confronting because they are conscientious and feel a personal obligation and responsibility not depending on others to fight their battles. Life of Riley? Yes. We all like to take it a little easier, shorter hours, etc. Maybe a hobby. Well, I guess all I can do at the present is to work, and dream sometime in the near future when I again can take out the fly rod, look up my flies and other gadgets and get away from this slapping of belts, hum and groan of laboring machinery and loiter along some quiet trout stream, but that time is not yet. In the meantime we have work that has to be done ere victory is won, and I think every true American will sense this obligation to do something at least, to prove they are Americans and contribute their part that we may retain our freedom which means our American way of life.

J. M. Kelley

Thursday, April 8, 1943

The Record-Post, Au Sable Forks, N. Y.

RONDEAU EXPLAINS REASONS FOR HIS WILDERNESS LIFE

Answers Article in This Paper by J. M. Kelley Relative to His Hibernating

In the March 18 issue of The Record-Post under the column "Public Forum" was an article by J. M. Kelley of Syracuse pertaining to Noah John Rondeau, the hermit of Cold River. Mr. Kelley in his article queried about the hermit's not taking any active part in the war effort. This week The Record-Post has received a reply from the Mayor of Cold River.

Says the hibernating hermit: "According to that article it is evident that one J. M. Kelley of Syracuse, broke out at the mouth and further used his quill or something else to launch before the reading public several malignant slaps at me directly. There are two parts in Kelley's article, as I see it. The main part, for scope, is to thrash me out and to set Kelley's stage for the second part of that article. The second part is for Kelley to blow Kelley's horn for Kelley. And the fact is, when the circumstances are known there is not one word of truth in all that Kelley wrote.

"The readers who happen to know me well enough to know the circumstances don't need further information. They knew before they finished the article that J. M. Kelley did not know what he was talking about. For the readers who don't know the circumstances Kelley's article leaves many false impressions such as that I'm hibernating at Cold River to dodge the war; I'm young enough, physically able, and I live the life of Riley, etc.

"Therefore, according to the circumstances for Kelley's knowledge of me no one could write what Kelley wrote and do it with any justification. Mr. Kelley also wrote that he is working long side men ten years my senior that are doing a real job. Well I have no criticism for men who just happen to be ten years my senior, and I'm not too sure that Kelley knows just what ten years my senior is. And as for 'a real job' I can't take Kelley's judgement seriously. If any man working at anything is not doing a better job than Kelley does as a writer it would be better for war or anything else if he was an old disabled hermit in the back woods minding his own business.

"Time and space does not permit one per cent of what I could answer Mr. Kelley on 'why does Mr. Rondeau have to hibernate at this time?' However, under the circumstances let a few statements suffice. I never went to Cold River to dodge anything, unless it was from 1930 to 1940 when it might be said I dodged the American labor failure at which time I could not get enough in civilization to get along even as well as I could at Cold River under hard circumstances in the back woods. Since I'm not evading I did not make my first appearance at Cold River on the day that Pearl Harbor was bombed.

"What I'm doing toward the war effort looks like nothing, but that's all I can do and I'm doing it and it is this —I'm self sustained. Not much to scream about I admit. I'm unable to go on a job, do worthwhile labor, put in the hours and be there the next day. I have done as much work as the average man of my age and I can still do some work. Otherwise I would have no business living at Cold River.

"A few times a year, I get concerned where I have to do a day's work—big enough for any man—and then it takes two days to get over it. Concerning my age, physical ability, etc., I wish as many have wished that it might be different. But what it is, is what it is.

Noah John Rondeau

Noah John Rondeau
Mayor of Cold River
Coreys, New York

April 8th, 1943

Miss Mary L. Colyer[1]
492B Hudson Avenue
Albany, N. Y.

Dear Young Happy—Mountain Climber

I was delighted to get Your Splendid Letter of March 30th. And I'm glad You and the Old Lady of Moab got the Cake and liked it.

It is true I ordered the Cake, But for the inscription, manner of Trim & etc. the credit belongs to The Old Lady of The Wigwam (Grace Hudowalski). I knew She would do a good job.

I was glad to get the picture, and will enclose herewith a scribbled page for Mrs. Menz. And say, the four in the picture—are not excaped Russian Refugees as You suppose. That's a nice young Indian Chief and three nice Old Squaws.

I'll let you in on it a bit, the way they got to the Mountain Top was eating bread and Candy and drinking Lemonade.

---

[1] Now Mrs. Adolph G. Dittmar, Jr.

The Young Chief Loves every one of the Squaws but He dont want anyone to know it,—so you wont tell; Thank You. The view and little hug on the Mountain Top was the climax; but it was a good day from beginning to end for The Indians.

On the way back you should have seen the ferry across the River—with a hop-skip and a jump over the Rocks. You should have heard the Silk rustle of Blue Denim and also, catch the difused odor of Happy-Medium-Blend-of Kerosene, Citronella and Pine-Tar. It was captivating beyond all power of resistance.

Well,—when we get better acquainted Dear, I'll let you in on The Beauty Parlor,—all about Indian Ablution and how They doll up.

Well, not much like Spring here yet, the crusted snow is two feet deep; Yesterday morning—10 below zero. And blizzards every day.

I've been set back this winter by several hard colds, and did not feel like starting out yet, for the 18 miles on snowshoes with a pack;—will soon make the lunge now.

And now closing—Good Luck to You Mary Dear. More Mountains and Valleys for You to explore; And more Pine Tar to You in fly time.

Sincerely yours,
Noah John Rondeau

March 20th, 1944
Town Hall, Cold River

Mrs. Grace L. Hudowalski
393 State Street
Albany, N. Y.

Dear Old Lady of The Wigwam:

I left Coreys Apr. 29th and after stopping at Ampersand Park I reached Cold River May 2nd (1943).

Have not seen The Post Office since, or even The

Gravel Road at Mountain Pond. My Mail came once (June 29th).

About fifty People called on me last year, which is a lot according to present war circumstances. Dr. Latimer and Attorney Gregory brought my Supplies as far as High Bank, Late in October.

Then I got a Medium Bear and a Ten Point Buck.

My last caller for 1943 went away Nov. 25th. Snow was over Twc Foot Deep at that time. Then I saw no one for nearly Four Months.

My first and only caller for 1944 so far, was a Lake Placid Beaver Trapper on Mar. 16th. Two of Them (Beaver Trappers) are at Moose Creek, and will call again before April. So I thought to write you a line which You may get in April.

I hope to go out in the next two Months and get my Christmas Cards and some Garden Seeds and Fish Hooks and Ration Points and License. Of course you understand without being told, I'm getting cityfied.

Well—The Hateful Dishonest American Flesh and Blood of The Conservation Commission has opened a Beaver Season for the last 17 days of March. But in the usual way of leading The Common People by The Nose —at The Hand of Big Business. No one knew before about Mar. 1st. And The Mayor knew when outsiders came and set Their Traps under His Nose.

The Great American Act of The Conservation Commission to "Open a Beaver Season" is worth no more to me than a German Mark, but its more hateful and grevious under the circumstances.

There were not many Great Outstanding City Events at Cold River in the last year. Several Visits were good, but usually very short.

One of The Outstanding Visits was Dittmar's for two days early in September, on Their Wedding Trip.

Christmas Day I had a Little Green Spruce planted in The Snow Bank in front of The Town Hall and a Little Deer came near Camp and fed about for 3 Hours.

April 19th, 1944

Well, I'm not much wiser than I was when I started this letter 4 weeks ago.

The Buck Deer is about all gone and I'm on my last can of Milk and I've been smoking Tea for 3 weeks. All this is not much trouble in camp. In fact no trouble at all.

Winter, I thought, was very mild, but long. Spring was mild so far, but gloomy and very little thawing. Snow is a foot deep in The Clearing; And throughout The Woods—2 to 4 feet of packed crusted snow. The only bare ground is Little Margin Patches of River Bank.

The River has not raised a foot above normal any time. So far as liquidizing The Snow and sending it down the River is concerned, it has hardly begun. My summer arrivers are—5 crows, 2 Song Sparrow, 1 Hawk, 1 Owl. 1 Duck, 1 Starling and today a handful of Brown Butterflies and 3 Robins.

* * * * * * * *

May 10th, 1944

Ampersand Park—I came here yesterday—from Town Hall, (city) Came through Ouluska; The last mile of climb on south side had plenty of snow—up to four feet. Elsewhere snow is about all gone. Spring is late, but lovely.

Grass is nice and green, here in the little clearing and at Town Hall. Only 5 kinds of Petal Flowers have opened yet. Catlins hang in bunches like Tassel. Pussy Willows have Kittens an inch long, with stamens and yellow pollen all around. Leaves have started in the last week.

My stay at Town Hall was 374 days.

Automobile tracks show the care taker has been at

the Pond. But I'm the only Mayor in the Park now. I found a note on the table—telling me where to find things—even a Blanket. I suppose the note was there for 6 months.

Rained all last night. Today rainy and very cloudy. Ampersand Mountain completely obscured.

I will walk to Coreys.

This is only a scribble from time to time on 6 year old paper—well smoked in the wigwam.

Noah John Rondeau

P. S. 4 p.m. at Coreys, N. Y.

May 11th, 1944
Noah John Rondeau
Mayor of Cold River
Coreys, New York

Dr. and Mrs. Adolph G. Dittmar
1320 Poppy Street
Warrington, Fla.

Dear Old People:

To start away back—on Sept. 6th, 1943 I launched You for Calkin Creek from the Balsams and Spruces at High Bank Cold River. I took my Pack to Town Hall; On the way I watched a Doe and a Fawn, slowly cross the River.

The Bride Flowers stayed on the Table in Mrs. Rondeau's Kitchenette for a week and a Pearly Everlasting from the Bouquet went into one of my Books as a Book Mark and hobby.

About Oct. 20th, Dr. Latimer and Attorney Gregory came to High Bank for ten days hunt. They brought in my supplies for Winter and after many back loads I got the supplies to the Town Hall.

Attorney Gregory got a 4 Point Buck and They went home happy Oct. 31st. Snow came and went for a while.

In November I got a Raccoon and a 10 Point Buck

and a 200 pound Bear. And 2 days after I got the Bear I could have killed another Bear; But "You understand" the law say "one Bear." Now if anything makes me mad —it's to see a Bear and can't shoot. In fact I was so mad I bit the top off from a little Spruce.

Nov. 21st, there was 6 inches of snow and that night it snowed a foot. Then snow kept packing and settling, but 3 or 4 times a week it snowed a few inches or a foot. By Christmas, packed snow was a yard deep. And then it was 4 feet. And it stayed a long time.

Christmas Day I had a little Spruce planted in the snow bank as a Christmas Tree and a little deer came to the Dam and fed around for 3 hours.

1944 came along and I had no license so I picked up my few Traps; I had no Almanac but I watched stars and planets and kept tabs on the Moon. By the time the calendar said "Spring" at Cold River among the major Adirondack Peaks, nights below zero still felt like winter and hard packed snow was 4 feet deep!

Then the Noble Crow came along.

It took all April to sweep the snow out of the Valley and up in the Mountains,—there is plenty of snow yet. The River and Brooks are high and Swamps are wet.

A dozen species of Birds have arrived and 6 kinds of Petal Flowers have opened up. Pussy Willows have Kittens an inch long with Stamens and Yellow Pollen all around. They look as if they might turn into Bumble Bees if they could grow wings. The Leaves have peeked out just enough to speckle the borders with green.

May 9th. I left Cold River and I came through Ouluska Pass. The last mile of climb to Ouluska had snow all the way—up to 4 feet—elsewhere no snow to bother. I reached the main road in Ampersand Park and found fresh Car tracks going to Main Camp at the Pond. So I went to the Pond—but found no one there except a Wild Rabbit on the Lawn. So I went back to the Guides Camp and rocked myself in Avery Rockefeller's Rocking Chair.

I found a note on the Table to tell me where to find food and even Blankets. I put in for the night.

May 10th was very cloudy. Ampersand Mountain was completely wrapped in Cloudy fog. And there were light showers.

I left a note on the Table and Midforenoon I left the Park Camp. And reached Corey's P. O. at 4 o'clock. Albert Hathaway came and got me at 6 o'clock. In the meantime I had supper with Hollenbechs at P. O.

I had all the Packages, catalogues, Newspapers, Letters and Christmas Cards that I could crowd into a large Nap Sack. We got to the Pine Point Camp at 7 o'clock. And after relaxing I went through my mail. I only went through it lightly and it took until after midnight . . .

My stay at Town Hall was 3 or 4 days; The Furtherest I got from Beauty Parlor was when I went to launch Newley Weds to Calkin Creek.

Well I got your 6 letters, cards, photos and News Clippings.

I'm told "The Forest Ranger at Chattock (Shattuck) Clearing—George Cole—died last winter."

I should write 40 letters but only have time for 5 or 10 at the most. And I must make a trip to Tupper Lake for Licenses, fish hooks and Garden Seeds.

On my last debut at Cold River I wrote 4 poems, in fact the last one is long and not finished—"Spring Time" which I'm writing now. And I wrote a manuscript (119 pages) of prose—my recollections of years ago: "A French Wedding in a Log House" when in type it will reduce to 40 pages. It's an outstanding Scream.

I will close, Thanking you for many Favors.

Very Truly,
Noah John Rondeau

WE THE PEOPLE

C B S Network
285 Madison Avenue, New York 17, N. Y.

April 11, 1947

Mr. Noah John Rondeau
Hotel Seneca
Rochester, N. Y.

Dear Mr. Rondeau:

We are considering the matter of inviting you to appear on "We, the People" again. So I would appreciate it if you'd keep me informed of your whereabouts during the next couple of months.

Mr. Clayton B. Seegers tells me you've been having a wonderful time—and that the same goes for the many thousands of people who've made up your audience. If you're not careful, you'll end up in the movies yet!

Best wishes and good luck.

Sincerely,
Walter Peters

* * * * * * * *

Adirondack Daily Enterprise April 12, 1947

Hermit broadcast: Hear ye, Hear ye—

This is Noah J. Rondeau, Adirondack hermit broadcasting with ink and quill and saying "Hear ye!" Just had a splendid visit in Ausable Valley. Gas buggied from Saranac Lake to Keeseville with W. E. Petty. After several calls at Keeseville I stopped for 24 hours at W. E. Clark's in Peru. At Clark's about 40 people called to see hermit; some were old friends I'd known long ago in Lake Placid or elsewhere. School youths and others came for autographs and several shot at me with loaded cameras.

Patches of sunshine tossed to earth between clouds. Distant mountains wore winter white, robins hopped across greening lawns and Spring was speeding on high around the corner screaming, "I'm bringing Summer in my rumble seat!"

Friend Clark gave me a book, loaded me with apples, tucked me into his gas buggy and took me to Ausable Forks. Here I took a day to catch up on my writing and 2 days to make 30 calls. Several had to be made within 10 minute period. Happy time with relatives, old friends and schoolmates of long ago.

Men and women seemed to be doing a lot of screaming about those young belles who kissed the hermit—even in those little places like New York City. Fact is that the old maids (and some other ladies) are jealous. The men have their noses out of joint because the belles won't kiss them. My answer is: to the ladies—seek and ye shall find. To the men—Raise pretty whiskers!

Noah John Rondeau

* * * * * * * *

Feb. 11th, 1948

Mrs. Marjorie L. Porter
100 Rugar St.
Plattsburgh, N. Y.
Dear Mrs. Porter:

I just got your splendid letter and its always pleasant to read your lines. Mr. Petty told me two weeks ago about "your resignation at Keeseville."

And Now,—a verse or two, semi confidential—I'm not sure that I will be at Cold River next season,—at least will be elsewhere part time; And you understand, —I must keep my franchise as a Hermit.

So,—I don't say very much about it. And you understand,—I will not be in the market to buy many airplanes—even when I get a Pilot's License. I have booked for the flying course ("if convenient") when the violets begin to bloom. And accordingly—my answer is "Yes" to your inquiry about me writing for "Homespun." And now,—you have the "Yes," and I don't know just how wonderful my writing will be but—whatever—it will be my best. And I will send you an appropriate copper plate to illustrate.

The News

I came out from Cold River City in late December. Have been at Saranac Lake most of the time. Had 6 days with Saranac Carnival: crowned the winter King and Queen—spoke at Trudeau's, spoke at Marcy Hotel, Lake Placid—at Fish and Game Club—Fish and Game Club dance,—Had first flying lesson—and first American Olympic Bobsled ride at Mt. Van Hoevenberg Bobsled Run.

And I pose 6 hours per week at Alpine Studio, for aspiring artists, who are painting the Cold River whiskers. The little local spirits are generally pleasant and the money generally lacking. Will have exhibition at Utica Sportsmen's Show next month.

And now,—closing—Thank you for many favors and your pleasant ways. And good luck to your carded wool, silk and fine yarn and threads for super weaving to climax in Homespun.

Noah John Rondeau

WE THE PEOPLE
285 Madison Avenue
New York, N. Y.

Dec. 7th, 1949

Mr. Noah J. Rondeau
4 Alpine Terrace
Saranac Lake, N. Y.

Dear Noah:

I want to thank you for your splendid performance and wonderful cooperation in making last Friday's WE THE PEOPLE such a successful one.

I hope the strain of all the rehearsals required by the combination broadcast and telecast was not too great; and that you left with a warm spot in your heart for we of WE THE PEOPLE.

If we can ever be of service to you, please don't hesitate to call on us, and again, many thanks.

Sincerely,
Jim
James Sheldon
Producer, WE THE PEOPLE

JS/cw

Old State Road,
Saranac Lake, N. Y.
January 11, 1951

Dear Mr. Rondeau,

I have been hearing about you for years (I have the Yearbook of the Adirondack Mountain Club for January 1939 containing an article about you, and your picture) and since I also am something of a hermit, I think we should meet. This can be accomplished only if you will come to see me, since I am an invalid and seldom leave the house in the wintertime.

For the past twenty years I have spent from four to six months of each year camping on Round Lake and Weller Pond. Once in camp I return to town only when I am compelled to do so, perhaps once or twice during the camping season. So you can see that I have lived a very isolated existence, and I think it would be interesting if we could "swap yarns."

My telephone number is 686-J—if you would like to call some time.

Very Sincerely,
Martha Rebentisch[1]

P. S. If you should get (what no hermit should ever get) an attack of the common cold, please delay your visit because I am functioning on only part of one lung and a cold puts me in bed for months.

[1] Martha Rebentisch (Reben) (1906-1966), resident of Saranac Lake for 39 years, was the author of three best sellers: THE HEALING WOODS (1952); THE WAY OF THE WILDERNESS (1956) and A SHARING OF JOY (1963).

February 12th, 1951
Noah John Rondeau
4 Alpine Terrace
Saranac Lake, N. Y.

Dr. A. G. Dittmar
Au Sable Forks, N. Y.

Dear Dr. Ditt:

Your letter came this morning. Thanks for the Letter and the Clipping; Yes—The Clipping is full of error But I'm used to that—no harm in this case; And after all; the Public will like that better than the real facts.

And now, I hasten to scribble because, tomorrow I will load Noah's Ark early and launch as far as Troy; And Wednesday I should reach Grand Central Palace about midday. Show Doors open Feb. 17th at 11 o'clock.

And about the Jay date: I suggest March 21st, And, keep the plan flexible so I can postpone if I have to.

New York is Big Advertising and its likely I may get another Show, lecture or Radio Program that I can't afford to turn down; And, if I have to postpone, I'll let you know as early as possible—and then, revive the occassion in April to over take the Jay Birds.

I hope this will not be disappointing to the Folks up Jay River; And just now it seems advisable to keep the plan flexible.

Thank you Dr. Ditt

Noah John Rondeau
Adirondack Hermit

OUR TOWN—Adirondack Daily Enterprise
by Eddie Vogt (4-4-51)

In flowing handwriting comes a letter from my good friend, Noah John Rondeau.

Dear Ed,

I observe that you observe that someone observes that

perhaps N. J. R. is out of town. Well, to make sure that we are all talking about the same fellow will say . . . The Noah Rondeau I know is a queer fellow. Sometimes he's a Dude in New York City, Grand Central district; sometimes he's a hermit in the sticks. Sometimes he smells of pretty perfume and sometimes it's just the odor of a woods animal. And he has whiskers not long enough for a primitive Moses but too long for a modern Airedale. Now the Mayor of the above measurements boarded the Greyhound Bus and went to Ausable Forks on Mar. 28th. And at 6 p.m. he went to Jay with Dr. Dittmar. At 7 o'clock he had supper with the Brotherhood Assn. of Jay and Wilmington. At 8 o'clock he listened keenly to the business meeting; from 9 to 10 he spoke to the Association as clever as Mitchall Micke Mick that swallowed the Blarney Stone. Mar. 29th at mid-day he dined with the Rotary Club at Ausable Forks and he spoke 35 minutes in a half hour. Mar. 31 he returned to Saranac Lake on the night bus and at the moment of scribbling he's at 4 Alpine Terrace.

Signed Noah Rondeau.

(E. Vogt's comment: Thanks, John, I've been wondering where you are)

July 6th, 1952—the day
I'm 69
Noah John Rondeau
Ausable Forks, N. Y.

Dr. C. V. Latimer
75 Front St.
Deposit, N. Y.

Dear Dr. Latimer:

I'm at Ausable Forks—came here the middle of May. I'm one mile out of town. Stopping with my Sister Mrs. Priscilla McCasland.

Her husband died 5 years ago—and she has 47 acres;

and I have taken over to some extent. I plowed 2 acres, bought 3 pigs, 1 sheep, 1 calf and 200 chicks.

One pig was last fall's shoat, quite big. I fed shoat and sheep grain for 5 weeks and I butchered them for mutton and pork. The rest of stock is doing well. Chicks mostly white leghorns are 6 weeks old.

Gardens are growing; so are the pig weeds. Potato bugs are raising hell. The worst trouble is—it's too much work for the old man.

And that's all the news on Hill Top Ranch near Ausable Forks.

Best regards to you and yours Dr. Latimer.

Noah John Rondeau

Rudolph G. Wiezel
Hamburg 1
Steunstrausse 5v

July 28, 1954

My Dear Reverend Rondeau:

Your exuberant message from the north woods after a judicious spell of silence was most welcome. You are, it seems, as vigorous and active as an enterprising showman should be. I am sure that behind all of the circus you are still able to convey some authentic Adirondackania to a few deserving and appreciative tourists. Our mutual friend Dutch Heil wrote me that over the 4th of July he ascended White Face the hard way (cooped up in a car seated behind the steering wheel) and regretted not finding (the hermit) about the exhibition grounds. He is taking things easy for a while at the advice of the doctor.

By the way, it is ten years ago just about this time, the last week of July, that we had the last powwow in the inner sanctum of the lodge before the great medicine man's own wigwam facing the rising moon that sailed high over Santanoni and Kuchakrage. For some reason or another we failed to take minutes of that meeting or give an interview to the press with the fatal result that the profound thoughts and opinions borne of that sombre yet August session are now irretrievably lost to posterity. All kidding aside, I realize that ten years with devastation of storm, fire in the woods and aging bodies have made a repetition of that evening impossible. It only serves to sharpen the memory of that and other moments in the more elusive retreats of the Cold River country.

While we are having a July of almost continuous rainfall, I read about the drought and heat in the States and fear that again the Adirondacks, especially the blowdown tracts are again in danger. What about that reported fire in the Cold River this spring? Was there very much to it? What gives with the Long Lake ranger, Russel; if you get in touch with him, give him my best regards.

Sincerely,
Weil

RONDEAU RHYMES

By now it should be fairly obvious that Noah John had quite a way with words. His "Recollections of 60 years," his journal entries and his correspondence all furnish ample proof of those phases of his versatility. Undoubtedly had he been able to get what he called a first-class education, he very likely would have made the most of his opportunities. Moreover, he later showed on numerous occasions that he could also speak as colorfully, convincingly and entertainingly as he wrote. But it is debatable whether more education would have made the verbal product more eloquent and effective than it now is. Formal training so often stifles and impairs inherent spontaneity of expression and the outcome often seems sterile and insipid.

Although there is no denying that Noey's poetry seems somewhat crude and rhymeless, it is nevertheless genuine and natural. While there is seldom any real attempt at any form of rhyme scheme or pattern it, in spite of the absence of traditional treatment, manages to communicate surprisingly well. There is no missing the message in "Living Among Hills," "To June," "To Mrs. Thomas Thomas," "Adirondack Winter," "Vernal Spring," "Message to Spring," "Information to September," and/or "To a Baby"—and that's more than can be said for many practicers of the poetic art. So many so-called poets seemingly do their utmost to confuse rather than turn on their readers.

Furthermore, there is little likelihood that anyone will ever accuse Noah of composing tasteless, "precious" morsels whose appeal and understandability are apparently directed toward a pre-selected and pre-conditioned clique or claque, whatever the case may be.

Incidentally, Noah personally had a pretty high opinion of his poems, but whenever he tried to get some newspaper publisher interested, his naturally shy efforts always met with a response that was anything but enthusiastic.* So, being almost supersensitive, he did not persist—even though he would have been satisfied with appreciative reception alone. Nevertheless, he continued to turn out poems. Sometimes these were jotted down on the backs of Morning Glory evaporated milk labels; sometimes on the blank areas of Xmas cards.

All told the originals—25 in number—contain 385 verses, 2068 lines and 16,500 words—by Noah John's own reckoning.

Besides the seven short ones that may be found in the Rondeau Journals, here is the more or less complete round-up of his poems: (1) Poetic Ideas, (2) To a Baby, (3) Spring Time, (4) On the Moon, (5) Adirondack Winter, (6) Jonah and the Whale, (7) Acrobatic Autumn, (8) Barefoot Girl, (9) Gregory and Rondeau, (10) When I Hop Off, (11) Peeps on Peeks on Mountain Peaks, (12) Late Spring—Early Autumn, (13) To Mrs. Thomas Thomas, (14) Random Scooter, (15) Information to September, (16) Allen's Bear Fight Up in Keene—Noah John's Reply, (17) Big Bear Lies, (18) Living Among Hills.

Uneven in quality and poetic concept though they are, his poems or poetic prose—clearly and favorably reflect the knowledge and nature of an intelligent, largely self-taught, perceptive and personable man—Noah John Rondeau, the Hermit of Cold River.

---

* See poem "Poetic Ideas" for names of newspapermen.

BR-RR-R-R IT'S COLD

(10-19-59)

Br-rr-r-r It's Cold
The topograph is one part green
One part soil color, and one part snow—
Br-rr-r-r it's cold!

Two Song Sparrows six feet from the door
Hop and pick in grass
Half covered with snow—
Br-rr-r-r it's cold!

Ground froze last night
Sunflower leaves are black
Boulders, a yard above grass
In the fields are white—

Br-rr-r-r it's cold!
Puddles of water have ice sheets
Covered with frost and
Morgan Mountain is Show of Snow
Br-rr-r-r it's cold!

TO JUNE

When I was a child,—
In New Mown Hay;
I caught odor of Sweet Grass
That often returns in Memory.

And after Autumn's Frost
Odors of frozen Ferns
Bring memories of that Child
In the New Mown Hay.

Now, in my old age,
I thank you June for thirty days;
That revive thoughts of odor of Sweet Grass
In Childhood's New Mown Hay.

GREGORY AND RONDEAU[1]

Before the Camera They Posed,
Before the Hunt begun.
Rondeau with a Bow,
And Gregory with a Gun.

Rondeau and Gregory—
Went Hunting on Monday
And Gregory said to Rondeau,
"Tomorrow will be Tuesday."

Rondeau said to Gregory,
"Of getting lost We need not fear,
We know right where We are,
That's very plain and clear."

Gregory said to Rondeau:
"We never get turned around.
We never use a Compass
And We never lose the Wigwam."

Rondeau said to Gregory:
"You took My Picture and sold it;
I can't forgive your Error,
And such Publicity."

Gregory said to Rondeau:
"I need Cartridges, and Fish Hooks too,
To get some Fish for Chowder,
And a Deer to make a stew."

Rondeau said to Gregory:
"Thy confession maketh me hungry.
Go in Peace—Thy Way—
And Hunt and Fish."

[1] Jay Lamont Gregory and his friend, Dr. C. V. Latimer, and their sons fished and hunted in the Cold River region for many years with Noah as their companion. Besides being a prominent insurance executive and civic leader in Binghamton, Mr. Gregory was also a well-kown amateur geologist. He died Sept. 19, 1947.

Gregory said to Rondeau:
"What makes You Pretty all the time?
Is it some hidden secret
That I might chance to find?"

Rondeau said to Gregory:
"What makes my Whiskers Shine?
I take Dr. Gregory's Vitamins,
During the Winter Time."

Gregory said to Rondeau:
"I comprehend so soon;
It's easy when you know,
Just like jumping on the Moon."

Rondeau said to Gregory:
"Fishing and Hunting make it clear
We must meet at the Wigwam
At least twice a year."

Gregory said to Rondeau:
"I'll be there twice a year.
With Wampums to get Fish
And Wampums to get Deer."

* * * * * * * *

ADDENDUM 1948

And now,—Rondeau says:
"Gregory, you've passed away.
You've left the Haunts and Hills,
You've ceased to hunt and fish.

I miss your corporeal ways,
And would miss, more dreadfully—
But I have you in vivid mentality
Of many, happy immortal memories.

From Beethoven, the words you wrote,
Are immortal as the words you spoke,
In Balsam Swamp, chasing Buck and Doe,
At Seward Pond, and Cold River Flow.

And Among mountains and vallies
While I live and hunt and fish.
You come daily and entertain
At campfire by Stream and Trail.

N. J. R.

* * * * * * * *

POETIC IDEAS

I know what I'll do to get rich quick;
I'll write poetry to make people happy;
And I'll sell it to Ed Bonville to publish
In the best paper in Northern Counties.

I never wrote many Canons of poetry;
But it will come easy when I get started.
I'll just write one line at a time,
And under, another, to make a rhyme.

And if I get a line down in the Grove,
I'll make it rhyme if it takes Black Brook;
And for Clintonville, what will not rhyme?
I'll take to Buck Hill, to Johnny Ryan.

And of the lines thats hard to match,
I'll make a bunch of this and that;
And fishing from Keene to Lower Jay,
I'll match all of them with specialties.

And if Jack Feulner don't like it,
It may be that George Cassavoy will;
And on the Jay Side, what will not rhyme,
Across the River, I'll put in Patrick Fyans.

I'll write milky ways, stars and galaxies,
Ologies, Little Brooks and great big Fish,
Fauna, Flora, High Mountains, deep Vallies,
Birds that stay, and Birds that migrate

My early recollections I'll write in rhymes
That will insinuate antique verve of ancient times,
And make the Reader, beautiful as a Poet's dream
When the Poet has a night mare in His sleep.

And on Palmer Hill—I'll write memories,
Of long ago, back in gay eighties;
Then I'll take Roger Nelson to Jackson Hill
Where at His age I used to play.

I'll write Jackson Hill — a rare story,
Before Automobiles, Air Planes and Radios;
When Raw Iron was hauled on planked roads
About the days Mose Ackey made Char Coal.

And there I'll write a verse or more,
About the Lilac Bush and Sweet Flag Root
I transplanted, more than fifty years ago,
From Dominac Amel's primitive abode.

And returning home Pigeon Hill,
If we meet Hank Noland at Franklin Shanty,
We'll stop and tell Him a thing or two
For taking my Apple in eighteen ninety-two.

Then I'll go down by the Old School,
And there I'll write an extra line or two;
And then walking over my Childhood route
I'll finish the verse chatting with Pettigrew.

Then on my way to the Fork of the River,
I'll write a verse to Mrs. Thomas Thomas;
The dearest Gammer ever born on Palmer Hill
Or who ever drank at Georgia's Spring.

And what will not rhyme, in Valley or Ausable,
I'll take to Champlain, to the Pipe Makers,
And with Frank Gibson and Billy Burger,
Write the Climax of another verse.

And when gold has bound the Lyric Volume,
And from Ed Bonville, I get my fortune,
At the Fork of the River, I'll build a Shanty
And put on a porch, with double wings.

There I'll retire for a Poet's happy old age,
With Flowers and rhymes, in varieties;
And, I'll get an Ausable Valley Old Maid
With a wart on Her nose and fuzz on her chin.

* * * * * * * *

LIVING AMONG HILLS

On carpet of leaves spread the year before,
Happy and often, I lay by a mountain brook—
And drank from a pebble trimmed natural cup,
Between little banks of living green moss.

And over the shady nook above the brook,
Among living green leaves that make the roof;
Through tiny holes, sunshine pours, light and gold,
That reach the brook like carded golden wool.

And the tranquil pool—by singing brook thrilled
Spin sunshine's golden thread in dancing skein,
Like supple acrobats on invisible trapeze,
Aquatic reflected on the rocks and trees.

Such are the Brooks in the shady nooks.
Where sunshine probes with bars of gold;
Which water pools into gold thread spin
That weaving ripples hang in dancing lace.

Here I watch the approach of fawn and doe,
Their glide so silent; I hear the trees grow.
They drink in shallow trimmed with golden lace,
Shaded by maples, alders and kinnickinnick.

Surrounding are the hills, with couches of rock,
Upholstered with moss, and garnished with grass,
Inhabited with fauna, in variety of life,
Over biological fossils, in geological rock.

Such are the hills with oak and maple.
Little Boys and Girls, acorns and syrup.
Rabbit and Grouse, Chipmonk and Chickadee
And a swarm of honey bees in a hallow tree.

Such are the hills, with variety of coats.
Their springtime buds make a purple show.
Early showers revive patches of grass and moss
And also the colors and perfume of flowers.

Then a coat of leaves—processing chlorophyll green
To beautify the hills and cool summer breeze.
And for bees, seeds for birdfeed and flowers to be.

Late summer brings russet, yellow and crimson,
But the climax of colors are for early autumn.
Then the leaves blanket the earth before snow,
And cuddle seeds that next spring will grow.

A late autumn night shrouds the hills with snow.
And morning reveals a strange brighter glow.
Snow on the Hills tattle the browsing deer's tracks.
And likewise the bear and the wandering fox.

The year's wardrobe for the hills are in varieties.
Swelling buds purple is appropriate to spring
Varying in sunshine, over maple clad hills
Just at the time the birds begin to build.

The best and most lasting is the summer green.
Making sugar with moisture, iron and sunbeams
In hills and vallies, habitat of man and beast,
Most dormantly peaceful and restful is vegetable green.

Beautiful but brief are colors of autumn leaves
That can't be fully explained but can be seen
Inexplicable by tongue or pen or reading in a den
One must gaze in season on hills and glens.

Winter's snow brings its evil and cold
But also its beauty and its gay winter sport
For many hold in remembrance of childhood,
A sled for Christmas and making a man of snow.

* * * * * * * *

LATE SUMMER

Well, well, is this September?
You was here last year, toward fall,
Where have you been since before October?
From where did you come, are you lost?

And you're escaping the Lion I see;
And the Virgin by the Hand you're leading,
Is it a marriage that you are seeking?
Or just taking the Sun, the South Pole to see?

And you came so quick, after August,
You have thirty days before October;
Beware of the Virgin because she's fickle.
When you take equal balance, you'll get the mitten.

Umbellate Asters and Gold Rods nod to you;
And the stage is well set to greet you;
Especially in north temperate latitudes
Much work's done and there's much to do.

Soft maples in Fens show red leaves;
And samples of yellow are on Birch Trees;
But the Forest is still generally green,
Awaiting your brushes, exquisite colors to reveal.

A multiplicity of seeds, many days growing
Are waiting your touches for browning;
Green Pumpkins are waiting your Gold,
And the Deer anticipate a new winter coat.

Artistic, the semi-circle of the Garden Gate,
Shoe-beaten foot trails are worn to polish;
Maturing Gardens among all things set quaint,
And late Flowers linger in summer beauty.

Cherries are ripe and Chipmonks are busy;
Cedar Birds take part and Crickets still sing,
The grass and shrubberies are tall by the way,
And rustic is the theme for Autumn Days.

* * * * * * * *

TO MRS. THOMAS THOMAS

1.

From Hermit Wigwams at Cold River,
A few verses to You, Mrs. Thomas Thomas;
Dearest Gammer ever born on Palmer Hill,
Or whoever drank at Georgia's Spring.

2.

Among rough contours, on precipice mountain slope
You was born long ago, exceeding purest Gold,
Hardly knowing, like perfume of a Flower,
Your spirit speaks sweeter than crowd can shout.

3.

Among drunken ruffins (ruffians), who sought to boast
The darkest deeds they dare explore;
Your boast was mute, but mentally felt,
For common things you loved the best.

4.

As dear as Stars that mark your sky,
Are little Bridges, Trees and Rugged Rocks
That mark your trails to Blue Berry Hills,
And to cool refreshing at Georgia's Spring.

5.

A season's fragrant flowers and sweet berries,
Like your youth is too brief and soon departed;
But Vallies garnished with Hill, your spirit unchained
Is shining symbol of the Boiling Spring.

6.

Many are your revolutions around the sun,
With Mother Earth on eastward orbital run;
Making varied seasons on tilted orbit,
As the Earth rotates, alternating night and day.

7.

You saw many seasons that come and go,
Winter's snow and fire in sunset glow,
Spring sunshine reviving summer green,
Then exquisite colors in Autumn Leaves.

8.

And the Lilac's Flora Spikes, bent with load,
Pointed your way on the country road;
As your journeys past the buck wheat field,
Honey scent you caught on summer breeze.

9.

You felt the ozone of summer evening,
And heard the Lark all night till morning;
You saw like day the moonlit sky,
And the moonless night with countless stars.

10.

Thoughts of you, as they often come my way,
Revive scenes of Jackson Hill and Franklin's Shanty;
Scenic Valley, all the way to Palmer Hill,
Oaks and boulders, Berry Pail and Boiling Spring.

11.

Dear remembrance from top of Palmer Hill,
Whose Maiden eyes distant scenes surveyed;
In gay eighties, among flowers of spring,
Beholding May robin on vernal wing.

12.

In the distance you heard the crusher roar,
And the metallic crash of dumping iron ore,
And you saw the kiln of charring wood,
And flaming glow of forge fires in blazing rows.

13.

Memories of you, like fragrant air, bless sweetly;
You got old, all but your spirit's best,
That's as sweet, beautiful and fresh
As Maiden and flower on Mountain crest.

14.

Per chance, a singular blessing for old age;
Cares and anxiety much time cause to vanish,
Leaving enduring beauty, pleasant in memory,
For happy meditation after many days.

15.

Your good spirit by our eyes unseen,
Reaches further than journey of your feet;
Like flower's perfume, unseen but sweet,
We love as sure as the flower we see.

16.

Not written for your funeral sermon,
But to bring you a happy living token;
Not fiction, but real as rocks on Palmer Hill,
Brooks and Vallies, you, and the Boiling Spring.

17.

Not lofty or in formal school refined,
Just a gifted soul, that few could divine,
Among hills and boiling springs, rain or shine
Your thoughts and words are immortal lines.

* * * * * * * *

WHEN I HOP OFF

If at my wigwam you find me dead
Don't start to whine then rant a prayer
To teach a myth, God will never know
That a Hermit died that never died before.

And don't get a coffin, trimmed with silver,
To preserve odor of my dead carcass,
And don't buy shining slippers to make believe
I'm jumping pearly gates with sprints from Galilee.

And don't burn candles near my head.
I hated paganism before I was dead;
And don't get Saint Peter, or Stovepipe Hat
Or Roman collar or Jack Ass Democrat.

Here are some ends that may be done
By common men, without uniforms.
Take birch and maple from my Wigwam
And build a fire on the ground.

And place my carcass on combustible bulk,
And cremate to vapor and to dust,
And the pale, bleached mineral of my bones,
Break to shale between rock and common stone.

Then rake coals and shales with wood I've cut
And finish burning near the Hut.
And leave me on top Cold River Hill
To repay to Earth my borrowed clay.

Then don't get bright, polished marble slab
And start to write the usual lies:
"I am not dead or awake, but sleep
And my harp I play at Jesus' feet."

Rather here is what is, without fiction's store,
The Hermit I was, I am no more.
While fire cremated, in a brief day
Nebulosity ascended while purified the clay.

And where I took off, near the Hut—
You'll find no such Hermit as I was;
All I leave of corporal real store
Is a bit of dust that was dust before.

And call it not hade or holy ground
Where shales of my bones are found.
Don't start a holy war at any time,
If someone plow and till the ground.

Stone not the Robin that seeks my clay
To build a mansion for coming babies.
Little Johnny shooting arrows chide not at all
Forbid not little Susie to play here with Her Doll.

Plants will come and bloom their flowers
And trees will grow to stately towers.
Fray not the Doe that nurses her Fawn,
Or Ruby Throat at the columbine.

* * * * * * * *

Although in this moving terminal poem Rondeau stated his strong desire to have his body become a permanent part of the soil of his beloved Hermitage, things did not work out as he devoutly wished. Instead, on August 26, 1967 he was buried in North Elba Cemetery which, while lacking the quality of remoteness, still commands a superb panorama of mountains, trees, valley and sky. A nearby line of pines, the Hermit's favorite tree, provides wind music for the infrequent visitor to this village of the dead.

There, in the shadow of the vault and within but a few feet of the grave of his friend Jacques Suzanne of dog team fame, were placed the remains of "a friend to the friendly"—the unforgettable, unforgotten Noah John Rondeau.

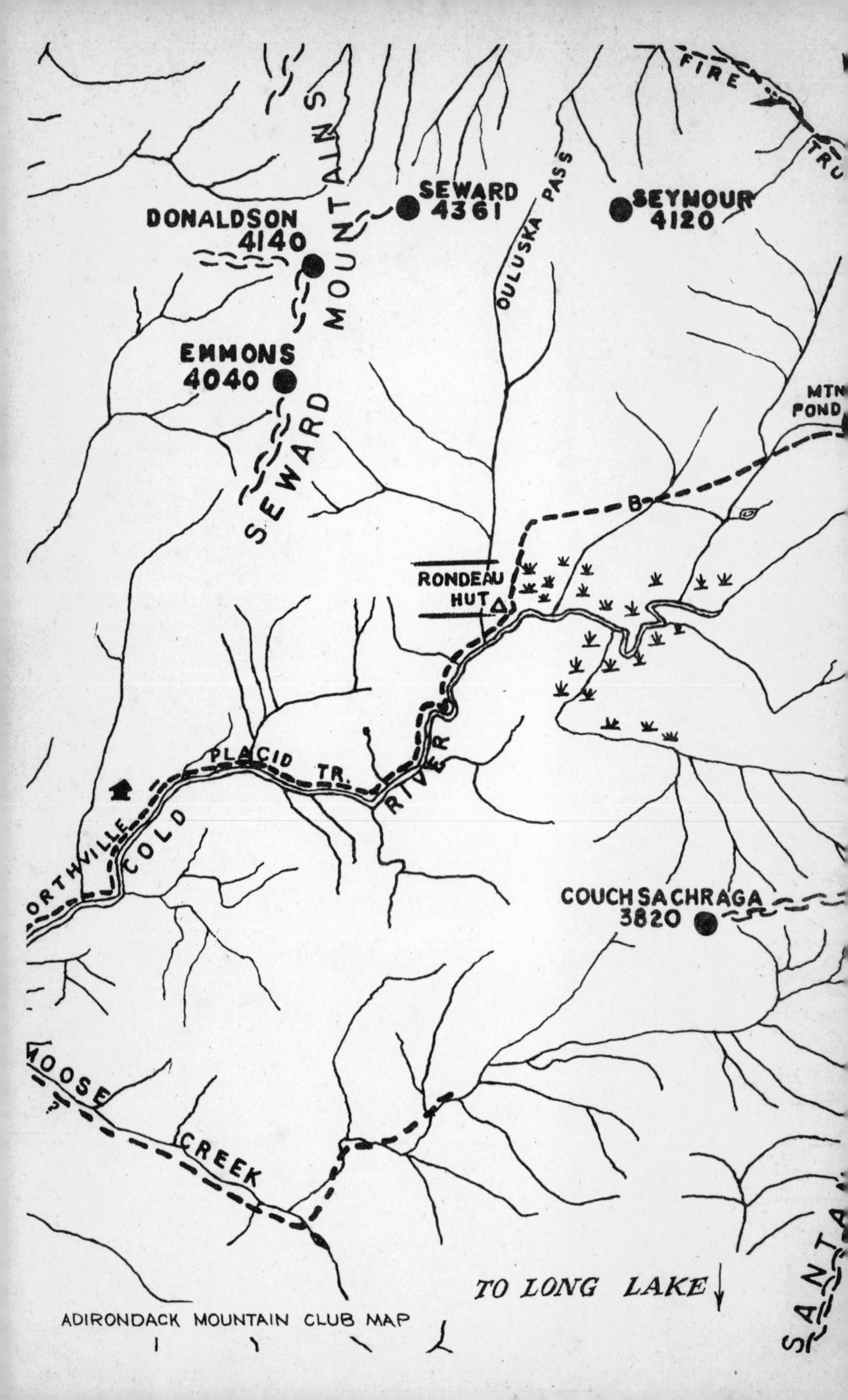
FIRE
TRU
SEWARD MOUNTAINS
SEWARD
4361
DONALDSON
4140
SEYMOUR
4120
OULUSKA PASS
EMMONS
4040
MTN
POND
B
RONDEAU
HUT
PLACID TR.
RIVER
COLD
NORTHVILLE
COUCHSACHRAGA
3820
MOOSE
CREEK
TO LONG LAKE
SANTA
ADIRONDACK MOUNTAIN CLUB MAP